CARIBBEAN
School Atlas
SKILLS WORKBOOK

Michael Morrissey

Name _____

Grade/Form/Class _____

School _____

Dedication

For my Caribbean grandchildren Kaelan, Katrianna, Kymore, Ksena, Jayden and Ashton.

Acknowledgements

The Publishers would like to thank the following for permission to reproduce copyright material.

Every effort has been made to trace all copyright holders, but if any have been inadvertently overlooked, the Publishers will be pleased to make the necessary arrangements at the first opportunity.

P.48 *tl* © Pietro Pazzi/iStock; *tr* © Oriredmouse/iStock; *bl* ESA, http://www.esa.int/spaceinimages/Images/2005/07/Envisat_image_of_ the_Great_Barrier_Reef_off_Australia_s_Queensland_coast, https://creativecommons.org/licenses/by-sa/3.0/igo/; *br* © Steven M Lang/ Shutterstock.com; **P.49** *l* © Paologozzi/Dreamstime; *r* © Frank Chen/Moment/Getty Images; **P.51** © Sergey Kelin/Shutterstock.com; **P.52** *tl* © Bob Thomas/Popperfoto/Getty Images; *tr* © AllOver images/allOver - Collection 005/Alamy Stock Photo *bl* © Franz Marc Frei/LOOK The stock photo agency Photographers GmbH/Alamy Stock Photo; *br* © Miles Davies/Alamy Stock Photo

Although every effort has been made to ensure that website addresses are correct at time of going to press, Hodder Education cannot be held responsible for the content of any website mentioned in this book. It is sometimes possible to find a relocated web page by typing in the address of the home page for a website in the URL window of your browser.

Hachette UK's policy is to use papers that are natural, renewable and recyclable products and made from wood grown in well-managed forests and other controlled sources. The logging and manufacturing processes are expected to conform to the environmental regulations of the country of origin.

Orders: please contact Hachette UK Distribution, Hely Hutchinson Centre, Milton Road, Didcot, Oxfordshire, OX11 7HH. Telephone: +44 (0)1235 827827. Email education@hachette.co.uk Lines are open from 9 a.m. to 5 p.m., Monday to Friday. You can also order through our website: www.hoddereducation.com

© Michael Morrissey 2019
First published in 2019 by Hodder Education (a trading division of Hodder & Stoughton Limited),
An Hachette UK Company
Carmelite House
50 Victoria Embankment
London EC4Y 0DZ
www.hoddereducation.com

The authorised representative in the EEA is Hachette Ireland, 8 Castlecourt Centre, Dublin 15, D15 XTP3, Ireland (email: info@hbgi.ie)

Impression number 10 9 8 7 6
Year   2025

All rights reserved. Apart from any use permitted under UK copyright law, no part of this publication may be reproduced or transmitted in any form or by any means, electronic or mechanical, including photocopying and recording, or held within any information storage and retrieval system, without permission in writing from the publisher or under licence from the Copyright Licensing Agency Limited. Further details of such licences (for reprographic reproduction) may be obtained from the Copyright Licensing Agency Limited, www.cla.co.uk

Cover photo © Shutterstock/Iakov Kalinin, Alamy/Sean Drakes, Alamy/foodfolio, Shutterstock/Sean Pavone

Illustrations by Integra Software Services Pvt. Ltd., Pondicherry, India.
Typeset in Integra Software Services Pvt. Ltd., Pondicherry, India.

Printed and bound by CPI Group (UK) Ltd, Croydon, CR0 4YY

A catalogue record for this title is available from the British Library.

ISBN: 978 1 5104 5995 3

CONTENTS

INTRODUCTION: ABOUT THIS WORKBOOK AND YOUR ATLAS 4
    Your *Skills Workbook* Glossary 5

PART 1   MAP SKILLS

1   MAXIMISING LEARNING FROM YOUR ATLAS 7
What is an atlas? 7
Types of map 8
Other kinds of information in an atlas 8
How an atlas contributes to learning 9

2   USING THE INDEX 10
The index is organised alphabetically 10
Practice in using the index 11

3   FINDING A PLACE BY ITS GRID SQUARE 12
What is a grid? 12
Follow four steps 13
Practice with grid squares 14

4   FINDING THE POSITION OF A PLACE BY ITS COORDINATES 16
Why are degrees used to state position? 16
Practice with lines of latitude 17
Practice with lines of longitude 18
Practice using latitude and longitude lines together 19

5   READING SYMBOLS ON MAPS 20
Point symbols 21
Line symbols 21
Colour tints on political maps 22
Symbols used for water features 22
Abbreviations 22
Practice in interpreting symbols 23
Practice with symbols 24

6   INTERPRETING LANDSCAPE 25
Colour tinting to show elevation 25
Colour tinting to show depth of seas and oceans 26
Spot height 27
Patterns affected by topography 27
Practice on elevation 28

7   STATING DIRECTION 29
Cardinal points of the compass 29
Intermediate directions 29
Make your own direction finder 29
How to use your direction finder, step by step 30
Practice in stating direction 30

8   WORKING OUT DISTANCE BY USING SCALE 31
What is scale? 31
Three ways of stating scale 31
Larger-scale maps and smaller-scale maps 32
Practice stating the scale of a map 33
How to calculate distance between two points 33
Practice estimating distance 34

9   GAME BOX: MAP SKILLS 35

10   MAP SKILLS TEST 38

PART 2   INTERPRET DATA, GRAPHS AND PHOTOGRAPHS

11   INTERPRETING DATA AND DIAGRAMS 40
Forms of data 40
    Information 40
    Fact files 40
    Tables 40
Practice in using fact files and interpreting tables 41
Diagrams 42
Practice in interpreting diagrams 43

12 INTERPRETING GRAPHS 44
Types of graph..44
    Line graph 44
    Pie graph..44
    Vertical bar graph....................................44
    Horizontal bar graph...............................44
    Pictorial graph 45
    Divided bar graph....................................45
    Flow chart 45
Practice in interpreting graphs 46

13 PHOTOGRAPHS....................................48
Types of photograph...48
Foreground, middle ground and background............49
Interpreting photographs....................................49
Practice interpreting photographs........................50

14 GAME BOX: DATA, GRAPHS AND PHOTOGRAPHS..52

15 DATA, GRAPHS AND PHOTOGRAPHS TEST...53

PART 3 INTERPRET THEMATIC MAPS

16 MAPS OF NATURAL PATTERNS..................54
Plate, earthquake and volcano patterns..................54
Topography..55
Seasons...56
Rainfall maps and graphs 56
Temperature maps and graphs 57
Climate and natural vegetation 58
Hurricanes..58
Environmental concerns....................................59
Time zones...59

17 MAPS OF HUMAN-MADE PATTERNS...........61
Historical movements of people 61
Population distribution......................................61

Administrative boundaries..................................62
Geographical regions..64

18 MAPS OF ECONOMIC ACTIVITIES 65
Tourism...66
Agriculture, mining and other economic activities.......66

19 GAME BOX: INTERPRETING THEMATIC MAPS... 69

20 TEST ON THEMATIC MAPS 72

PART 4 ACQUIRE PLACE KNOWLEDGE

21 KNOW YOUR OWN COUNTRY 74

22 KNOW THE CARIBBEAN REGION............. 76
What is the Caribbean region? 76
Independent or belonging to another country? 76
What is the Caribbean Community? 77
Make your own map..78
Flags of the Commonwealth Caribbean...................78
Make a display of maps of Caribbean countries..........80

23 KNOW YOUR WORLD 81
Continents 81
Countries of the world......................................82
North America...83
South America...83
Europe..83
Africa..84
Asia..85
Australia and the Pacific.....................................85
The world's capitals...86
Oceans, seas and lakes 87
Earth as a planet of the solar system......................88

24 GAME BOX: KNOWLEDGE OF PLACES........89

25 PLACE KNOWLEDGE TESTS....................92	
Caribbean knowledge 92	
World knowledge 93	

SELECTED OUTLINE MAPS

North America..95	Caribbean hurricane tracker chart........................100
South America 96	Africa..102
Europe 97	
Caribbean countries..98	

Your online map bank

Complementing this workbook is an online resource of outline maps. These can be downloaded and printed for use with exercises in this workbook. The webpage is www.hoddereducation.com/atlasworkbook. You will find a special icon beside some of the exercises in part 4 of this workbook. This reminds you to open the webpage, find the required outline map, and print it.

ONLINE MAP BANK

Maps of Continents
North America
South America
Africa
Europe
Asia
Australia and the Pacific
Oceans, seas and lakes
Continents challenge

Caribbean region maps
Caribbean countries
Caribbean hurricane tracker chart
Countries of Central America

Caribbean country maps
Antigua and Barbuda
The Bahamas
Barbados
Belize
Dominica
Grenada
Guyana
Jamaica
St Kitts and Nevis
St Lucia
St Vincent and the Grenadines
Trinidad and Tobago

Introduction: About this workbook and your atlas

This workbook is designed to help you acquire Social Studies, Geography and History skills through your atlas. These are skills related to the interpretation of maps, data, graphs, diagrams and photographs. Exercises will increase your knowledge and understanding of places in the Caribbean and the wider world. All the information you need for exercises in this workbook can be found in the Hodder Education *Caribbean School Atlas*. All atlas page numbers in this workbook refer to the 2018 edition.

Every time you use this workbook you should have your atlas beside you. Your atlas is a treasure chest of information!

Your *Skills Workbook*

Key words and terms

Each term related to map skills, such as the word atlas, is given in bold type the first time it appears in the workbook. The terms are listed in alphabetical order in the Glossary on pages 5–6. When you first come across a key word, look it up and read the definition. When you have finished all the exercises in this workbook you should be able to explain all the words listed in the Glossary.

Map skills

In the first two parts of the workbook, you will acquire and practise map skills such as finding direction and calculating distance.

Interpreting thematic maps

Parts 3 and 4 will help you understand and make good use of atlas maps on special themes or topics. Maps about climate or tourism or the environment of a place are examples of these.

Graph and photograph interpretation skills

Your atlas also has photographs that complement some of the the maps. You will learn to interpret how much can be revealed by a photograph.

Knowing the world in which you live

You will get to know aspects of your own country and region, the wider world and solar system.

Space is given for every answer. You will need a set of coloured pencils (red, green, yellow, blue, orange and brown are useful). These coloured pencils are for shading maps and flags.

Special symbols and fonts are used throughout the workbook to help you:

 This symbol is at the beginning of each chapter to tell you what you will learn.

 This symbol reminds you to get active and complete the task set.

 You may also see this symbol, which suggests that you try the exercise in a small group with other students in your class.

 When you see this it is time for a quick quiz to test whether you have acquired the new skill.

 This symbol appears next to critical thinking/problem solving tasks. These are to encourage you to think creatively using the atlas data. There is no single solution to such tasks. Your classmates might come up with solutions different from your own.

 This symbol tells you to go online and print the outline map needed for this exercise.

elevation words appearing like this remind you to turn to a definition in the Glossary and make sure you understand the meaning of the special word or term.

page 48 page numbers like this remind you to turn to these pages in your atlas and look at them alongside the workbook.

GLOSSARY OF WORDS AND TERMS

The list below gives definitions of words and terms that you will need as you develop your map skills.

administrative division How a country is divided into regions for local government; sometimes called political divisions.

archipelago A group of islands arranged in a line or a chain.

atlas A book of maps designed for a specific group of users. The *Caribbean School Atlas* is designed for students in primary school and the early grades of secondary school.

bar graph A graph made of bars, arranged horizontally or vertically, the length of each one equivalent to the amount portrayed; also called a bar chart.

biodiversity The multitude of animal and plant species living in a particular habitat.

boundary An imaginary line that separates two countries or two administrative areas.

capital An urban area, city or town that is the chief administrative centre of a country or one of its administrative areas.

cardinal point A principal point of the compass; there are four: North, East, South or West.

colour tint Shading to show a country or a pattern on a thematic map.

compass rose A symbol on topographical maps to show the cardinal directions.

continent One of planet Earth's seven major landmasses.

coordinate The intersection of a line of latitude and a line of longitude, providing a pointer to where a place is located.

direction The whereabouts of one place from another, using cardinal points.

elevation The height of a place above sea level, stated in metres in this atlas; also called altitude.

Equator The line of latitude 0 degrees (0°) that circles planet Earth midway between the North Pole and the South Pole; it is a great circle, the maximum diameter of Earth.

flow chart A diagram in which the width of the flow line illustrates the volume of what is moving from one point to another.

globe A model of planet Earth.

Greenwich Meridian The line of 0 degrees of longitude, which passes through the town of Greenwich in London, England. Also called the Prime Meridian.

grid line A line of latitude or a line of longitude on a map.

grid reference A reference that identifies a point or a grid square on a map.

grid square A square enclosed by two lines of latitude and two lines of longitude.

hemisphere Half of a planet.

hurricane tracker chart An outline map designed to plot the movement of a hurricane.

index A list showing words in alphabetical order. In the *Caribbean School Atlas*, the index provides a page number for each place listed and a grid reference to help you find the place.

intermediate points The directions in between the cardinal points of direction.

key The explanation of colour tints and other symbols used in a map; sometimes called the legend.

languages map Shows languages spoken in a continent, country or region.

large-scale map A relatively small area shown at a scale that allows detail.

letter–number coordinates The grid square at the intersection of a line of latitude designated by letter and a line of longitude designated by number (e.g. A2).

line graph Points plotted on a graph joined by a line or lines, usually showing changes over time.

line of latitude An imaginary line circling Earth easterly–westerly and parallel with the Equator (which is 0 degrees of latitude).

line of longitude An imaginary line circling Earth northerly–southerly, passing through the North Pole and the South Pole.

location The position of a place.

map A map is a careful drawing of a specific area, such as a country, a continent, a district or a city, to show its main features as these would appear if looked down on from above.

North Pole The point in the Earth's northern hemisphere that forms the north end of the axis upon which the planet rotates.

North Point One of the cardinal directions.

orbit The path of a planet around its sun, or of a moon around its planet.

outline map Shows a place in outline; drawn so more detail can be added.

photograph interpretation The skill of gathering information from a picture to identify all that is shown.

physical map Shows natural features, such as hills and rivers (not the patterns made by humans); also called a relief map.

pie graph A circle, divided in sectors according to the way the percentage of the whole is being illustrated; also called a pie chart.

planet A large sphere that revolves around a star.

political map Shows the boundaries of countries or regions and the administrative capitals.

population density How many persons live per square kilometre.

population distribution How the population of a country is spread.

population pyramid A type of bar graph showing percentages of the population by age group and gender.

Prime Meridian The line of longitude numbered zero degrees (0°). This is internationally agreed as the base line for positioning all other lines of longitude. Also called the Greenwich Meridian.

rainfall graph Shows average rainfall of each month of the year, usually as a bar graph.

rainfall map Shows how much rain falls in different parts of an area, usually by colour tinting.

ratio scale The scale of a map expressed as a ratio, such as 1:25,000. Also called a representative fraction when written in that format, for example 1/25,000.

region An area that shares common characteristics of landscape or human activities or an area designated as a unit for administrative purposes.

relief map Shows how high or low the land is (its elevation), usually by colour tinting.

resources map Shows natural resources and economic activities, including the agricultural, mineral and other aspects of its economy.

road pattern How roads are organised in an island or region.

rotate The spinning movement of a sphere on its axis.

scale The relationship between a line on a map and the distance on the ground, expressed as a ratio scale or line scale.

scale bar The scale of a map shown by a horizontal line and equivalent distances.

small scale A map of a large area at a scale that does not allow detail to be shown.

solar system The star called the Sun and its eight planets, including Earth, and their moons.

South Pole The point in Earth's southern hemisphere that forms the southern end of the axis around which the planet rotates.

spot height A point on the surface of Earth whose elevation is stated in metres above sea level.

statistical table A way to show information organised in columns and rows.

symbol A colour, shape, line, number or letter representing something on a map.

temperature graph Shows how temperature varies over the months of the year, shown in the *Caribbean School Atlas* in degrees Celsius (°C).

temperature map Shows how average temperatures vary over the area shown.

thematic map Shows information about a particular topic or topics, e.g. the patterns of hotels and tourist attractions in Tobago. Also called a topic map.

time zone A north–south band of planet Earth with the same time. Each band theoretically covers 15 degrees of longitude. Noon occurs in the middle of the period of daylight for each time zone. Each country decides on the exact positioning of its own time zones.

topographic map Shows relief and rivers. Sometimes also includes roads and settlements. We interpret the landscape by reading a topographic map.

tourism map Shows aspects of the tourism industry, especially where hotels are located and the attractions that tourists enjoy.

world map Shows the entire planet Earth on a flat sheet of paper.

1 Maximising learning from your atlas

PART 1 **MAP SKILLS**

1 Maximising learning from your atlas

> 🔒 **NEW SKILL**
> Recognise that atlas-associated skills are key to learning about your country and the world.

Students studying Geography and Social Studies for Caribbean examinations will need a more detailed atlas. Remember: every atlas is specially designed for a specific audience.

Each map shows a specific area, such as an island, a **region**, a **continent** or the whole world. At the top of each atlas page, the title states which place is covered and what are the topics. Individual maps on each page are captioned to state what is covered.

In addition to maps, an atlas includes diagrams and graphs that elaborate on what the maps show. In an atlas for young people, like the *Caribbean School Atlas,* there are also photographs that help you to visualise what the maps are showing.

Reading an atlas is different from reading a book. This workbook is designed to give you new reading skills – how to read maps! Let's begin by looking at the way information about Trinidad and Tobago is presented on atlas **pages 48 and 49**.

What is an atlas?

The Hodder Education *Caribbean School Atlas* begins with the question 'What is a map?' (see **page 2**). Work through the eight illustrations and the caption beneath each one. This page will help you to understand how maps are designed for an **atlas**, step by step. Turn to the Glossary on **page 6** and read the definition given for the term **map**.

You can see by looking through your copy of the *Caribbean School Atlas* that an atlas is a collection of maps assembled for a specific purpose. The maps selected for this atlas relate to Social Studies topics that young people across the Caribbean focus on in primary school and at the beginning of secondary school.

> ⏰💬 Look at atlas **pages 48 to 49**. In your group, discuss the different ways information about Trinidad is shown on these pages. You will also notice different types of map.

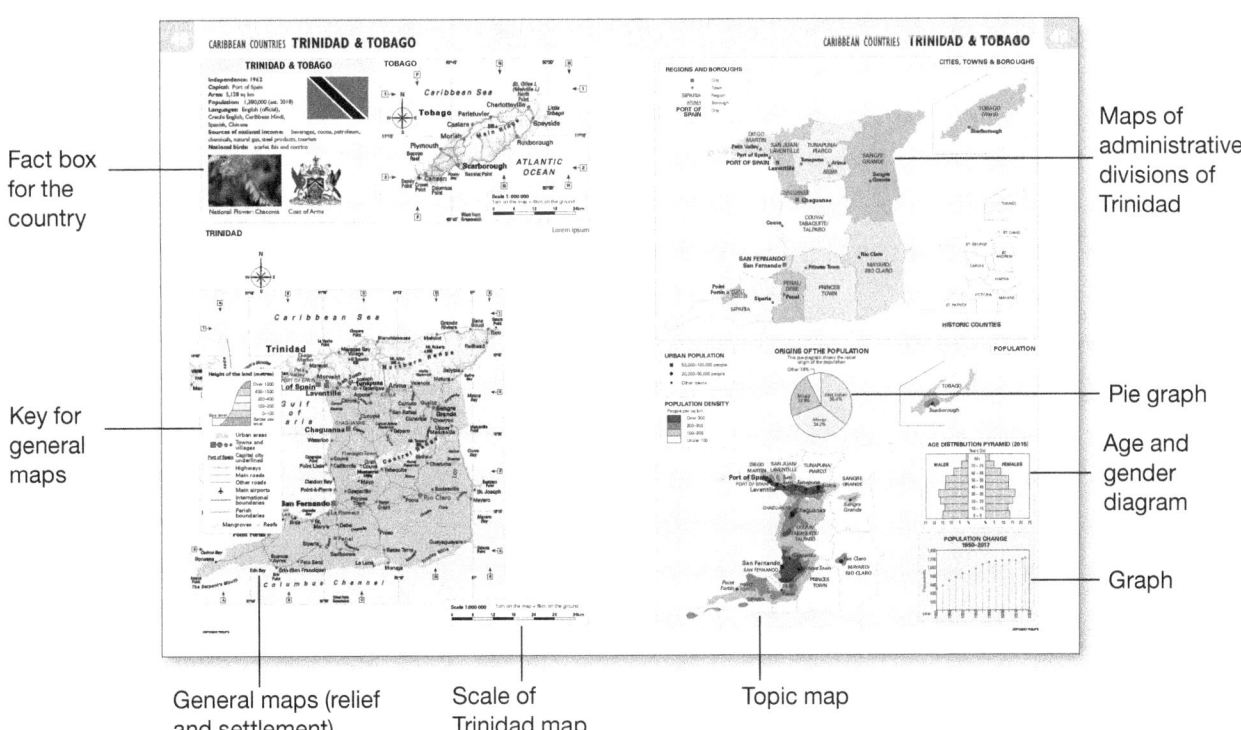

- Fact box for the country
- Key for general maps
- General maps (relief and settlement)
- Scale of Trinidad map
- Topic map
- Maps of administrative divisions of Trinidad
- Pie graph
- Age and gender diagram
- Graph

PART 1 MAP SKILLS

Types of map

Let's now look at the Barbados maps on atlas **pages 46 to 47**. You will see a **topographic map** on **page 46** that shows physical features (hills, plains, rivers, coastline) and human development (roads, towns, urban areas, parish boundaries). There is a **political map** in the left lower corner of **page 46**, showing the **administrative divisions** of the island. There are also four **thematic maps** of Barbados, each showing a different pattern. Your next task is to recognise these themes.

> On **page 47**, maps show four different themes. Point to the one that shows:
> - areas of low and higher rainfall
> - how economic resources are distributed over the island
> - which parts of the island are densely settled and which parts are almost unpopulated
> - areas where most tourists stay and the attractions they enjoy.

A map that shows physical features alone is called a **physical map**. You will find examples of physical maps for each of the continents on **pages 60, 62, 64, 66, 68 and 71**.

On **page 3** of your *Caribbean School Atlas* the term thematic map is explained in detail. Five examples are given. Read about each theme.

There is no limit to what themes can be shown by maps as long as the subject is something that differs from place to place over the area shown in the map.

> Look at the following atlas pages and write down which themes are covered in the maps.
>
> 1 What are the specific themes on **page 17** that show aspects of the Caribbean region's population?
>
> ....
>
> ....
>
> ....
>
> 2 The thematic map for Belize on **page 23** covers the following three themes:
>
> ....
>
> ....
>
> 3 Themes covered in maps on **page 32** are:
>
> ....
>
> ....
>
> 4 The four thematic maps of Guyana on **page 55** cover:
>
> ....
>
> ....
>
> 5 World themes covered in maps on **page 83** are:
>
> ....
>
> ....

Other kinds of information in an atlas

A school atlas includes diagrams, graphs and photographs related to the information displayed in topographic and thematic maps. These are to help you to understand what is shown in the maps and to provide additional detail. Let's look at examples of each of these.

> Complete the following sentences about the kinds of atlas content other than maps by selecting the correct option from the three provided.
>
> 6 Under each photograph in the atlas is a
>
> ....
>
> (number, caption, name of photographer)
>
> 7 Monthly rainfall is shown on **pages 23, 31 and 78** by ....
>
> (bar graphs, line graphs, thematic maps)
>
> 8 How a volcano erupts is explained on **page 81** by a ....
>
> (graph, photograph, cross-section)

How an atlas contributes to learning

This diagram is in the inside front cover of your atlas. It demonstrates the value of your atlas in learning topics you cover in school.

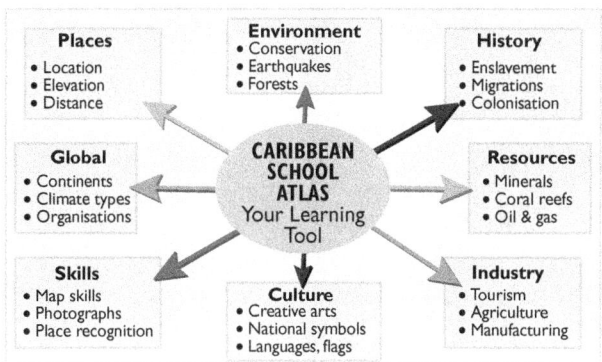

There are three bullet points for each of eight topics shown in the diagram. With a partner, see how quickly you can find one example of a map or diagram that gives information about each topic listed. You can write your answers in the table below. The first sub-topic is started for you as an example.

Begin by writing in another example of a map of a continent. Put your example in the box under the example provided.

Topic	Sub-topic	Map or diagram in the *Caribbean School Atlas*	Atlas page
Global	Continents	Physical map of North America	60
	Continents		
	Climate types		
	Organisations		

PART 1 MAP SKILLS

QQ Quick quiz on the meaning of atlas

Select the correct response for these quiz questions about an atlas. Tick a, b, c or d.

1. An atlas is:
   a. a body-building competition named after Charles Atlas
   b. a journal with a traveller's tales from around the world
   c. a collection of information in the form of tables
   d. a book comprising maps of different places

2. Which of the following kinds of map is not found in your *Caribbean School Atlas*?
   a. Political maps
   b. Bus route maps
   c. Physical maps
   d. Topographic maps

3. The following is an example of a thematic map:
   a. Rainfall graph
   b. Temperature graph
   c. Rainfall map
   d. Hurricane photograph

4. The colour tint at the top of each page of your *Caribbean School Atlas* shows:
   a. the content of a page
   b. which day of the week to use the page
   c. the section of the atlas
   d. which country the page is about

5. Why are photographs included beside maps on many pages of your atlas?
   a. To provide complementary information to that which is shown on maps
   b. As advertisements placed to see something while you are using your atlas
   c. To make the atlas attractive to buy
   d. To fill empty space on a page

2 Using the index

NEW SKILL

Learn how to quickly find the location of a place by using the atlas index.

To begin atlas skills, you must practise the important skill of using the atlas **index**. The index enables you to quickly find places in the atlas. The *Caribbean School Atlas* has an index of places on **pages 86 to 89**. This lists places shown in the atlas.

The index lists all the countries of the world and their **capital** city. You may be looking for a physical feature, such as an island, a mountain peak, river or lake. These are listed. Or you may be looking for the **location** of a human-made feature such as a country, a city or a town. You will find these too.

In summary, this is what is listed in the atlas index:
- physical features of the landscape such as islands, reefs, mountains, highlands, hills, peaks, ridges, peninsulas, reefs, deserts
- water features such as oceans, seas, rivers, lakes, passages between islands, gulfs, bays
- human features such as capitals, cities, towns.

Use the index to see how quickly you can find the name of your own country and its capital city.

The index is organised alphabetically

All names in the index are listed in alphabetical order. But some names include a descriptor for the kind of feature it is (for example, the Gulf of Paria, to the west of Trinidad). Its place name is in alphabetical order followed by the description:

Paria, Gulf of

Sometimes, the same name occurs in more than one country. In these cases, the country names

2 Using the index

are added after each place name, and they are in the index alphabetically by country.

For example:
Richmond *Jamaica*
Richmond *USA*

All river names are shown in blue (without the word river). Look, for example, for a river in Guyana:
Demerara

Every name in the index is followed by the page number of a map it appears on, and then a letter and a number.

For example: Chaguanas 48 C2.

The best map to find Chaguanas is on **page 48**. C2 is its **grid reference**. The use of grid references is explained in the next chapter.

All these place names are arranged in alphabetical order (a, b, c). This makes it easy for you to search for a specific place name. This next exercise will help you to remember that places are listed alphabetically.

> Put the following place names in alphabetical order. You do not need to use your atlas.
>
> 1. **a)** San Juan **b)** Anguilla **c)** Tortola **d)** Cuba
>
>   ....
>
> 2. **a)** Bridgetown **b)** Belmopan **c)** Black Sea **d)** Basseterre
>
>   ....
>
> 3. **a)** St Vincent **b)** St Barthelemy **c)** St Kitts **d)** St Lucia
>
>   ....
>
> 4. **a)** Caribbean **b)** Caracas **c)** Carriacou **d)** Carlisle Bay
>
>   ....

To write these place names in alphabetical order, each exercise made you do something different.

In Question 1 you had only to look at the first letter, as each word began with a different letter.

In Question 2, all began with 'B', so you used the second letter of each to put them in order.

In Question 3, the first two letters were the same for each place, so you used the third letter.

In Question 4, all began with 'Car', so you had to use the fourth letter to put them in order. This is how an index works!

Practice in using the index

> See how quickly you can find the atlas page number for each of the following Caribbean countries. Do not write in the grid reference, just the atlas page number.
>
> 5. St Lucia: page ....
> 6. Jamaica: pages ....
> 7. Cuba: page ....
> 8. Turks and Caicos Islands: page ....
> 9. Trinidad and Tobago: page ....
> 10. Haiti: page ....

> Find the following cities in the index and write the name of the country each one is in.
>
> 11. Yangon. Country: ....
> 12. Tokyo. Country: ....
> 13. Port-au-Prince. Country: ....
> 14. Kiev. Country: ....
> 15. Addis Ababa. Country: ....

> Use the index to find the places named in the following questions. Then complete the sentences.
>
> 16. Costa Rica is a .... in the continent of .... It lies between Nicaragua and ....
>
> 17. The Essequibo is the major .... of ....
>
> 18. St George's is the .... of ....
>
> 19. The two .... of Antigua and .... together make up a single ....
>
> 20. Zambia is a .... in the continent of ....

PART I MAP SKILLS

⏰ Find the four cities of the twelve listed below that are capital cities. Capital cities are shown on the map by a special symbol, a red square.

Santiago, Cuba	Kingstown, St Vincent	Berlin, Germany	Shanghai, China
New York, USA	Toronto, Canada	Riga, Estonia	Rio de Janeiro, Brazil
Warsaw, Poland	Cape Town, South Africa	Mumbai, India	Dar es Salaam, Tanzania

21 The four cities that are capitals of their countries are:

....

....

QQ Quick quiz about the index

Use the index of your *Caribbean School Atlas* and circle one place name that is wrongly classified in each list.

22 Countries:	Thailand	Tasmania	Swaziland	Sweden
23 Islands:	Grand Turk	Little Cayman	Bequia	Basseterre
24 Rivers:	Odessa	Rio Minho	Corentyne	Rhine
25 Capitals:	Libreville	Lilongwe	Lima	Lithuania
26 Towns that are not country capitals:	Port of Spain	Portsmouth	Ponce	Port Antonio

3 Finding a place by its grid square

 NEW SKILL

Learn how to find the location of a place on a map by using the letter-number coordinate given in the index.

What is a grid?

On every topographical map in your *Caribbean School Atlas*, you will see horizontal and vertical lines. The horizontal lines are oriented east-west. The vertical lines are north-south. These lines are referred to as **grid lines**.

Where two adjacent horizontal lines cross two adjacent vertical lines, a rectangular shape is formed. This is called a **grid square**. A grid square is an area on a map bounded by four grid lines.

Although we call these squares, you may observe, when you look at one, that they are not truly square. This is because planet Earth is spherical, and vertical grid lines taper as they near the North or South Poles.

These east-west and north-south lines are lines of **latitude and lines of longitude**, which you will learn more about in Chapter 4.

Between each north-south line you will see a letter. Between each east-west line you will see a number. These **letter-number coordinates** are shown in yellow squares along the edges of a map.

Here is an example from Trinidad. The index tells you that you will find the town of Chaguanas at **48 C2**. This means that on **page 48**, Chaguanas lies somewhere in the grid square in which C is crossed by 2.

3 Finding a place by its grid square

Please note the following indexing rules:
- Towns are indexed according to the grid square where the town symbol is – not where its name is.
- Rivers may cross many grid rectangles, so the index refers to the square where the river is named nearest to the sea.
- An area such as an island, mountain range or country may fall into more than one grid rectangle. The rectangle given in the index is the centre of the area named.

Follow four steps

Here is an easy way to find a place. Let's find the parish of Hanover in Jamaica. It is shown in the index as **Hanover 26 B2**.

To find this parish, open your atlas on **page 26** and follow these four steps:

Step 1. Put the index finger of your right hand on the correct letter along the bottom edge of the map.

Step 2. Put the index finger of your left hand on the correct number at the left side of the map.

Step 3. Move your right-hand index finger upwards and your left-hand index finger to the right on the map.

Step 4. Your two index fingers will meet in the grid square B2.

You will have found the parish of Hanover!

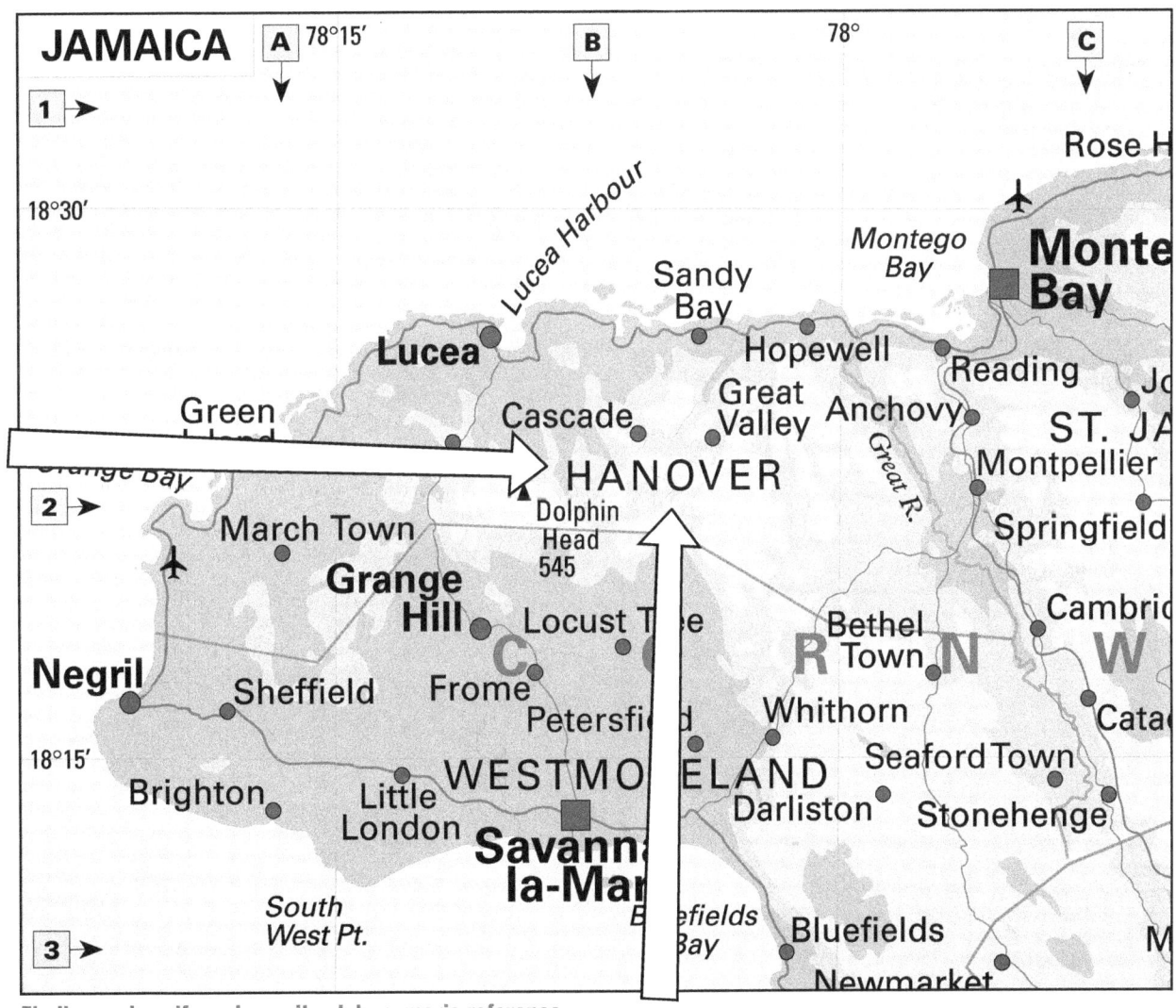

Finding a place if you know its alphanumeric reference

PART 1 MAP SKILLS

Practice with grid squares

Below is an outline map of St Lucia with grid lines. Now look at the atlas map on **page 42** and fill in the correct letter–number grid reference for the each of the squares numbered 1 to 5 on the outline map.

1 .... 4 ....

2 .... 5 ....

3 ....

Map of St Lucia

Use the index to find in which country the following places are found.

6 Santo Domingo ....

7 Port-au-Prince ....

8 Vieux Fort ....

9 Fort-de-France ....

Now find the name of the capital city of:

10 St Lucia ....

11 Trinidad and Tobago ....

12 Panama ....

13 Belize ....

3 Finding a place by its grid square

> Different Caribbean countries often use the same place names. Find the same place name in each of the following pairs of countries. Begin by using the index to find the most detailed map of each country. The grid reference for each place is given after the country name.

14 St Vincent C2. Guyana B2 ....

15 Saint Martin A1. Dominica B1 ....

16 Dominica B3. St Lucia A2 ....

17 Guadeloupe B4. St Kitts B2 ....

18 Jamaica G4. British Virgin Islands H2 ....

> Look at the map of Belize on **page 23** and write down the number-letter grid square where the following features are found.

19 The Turneffe Islands of the Barrier Reef ....

20 The capital, Belmopan ....

21 Belize's highest peak ....

22 The international airport ....

23 Where the Belize river enters the sea ....

24 Boundary to the south of Belize and Guatemala ....

25 Most of Stann Creek district ....

26 The Northern and Southern Lagoons, south of Belize City
....

27 A grid square that has parts of three countries (Belize, Mexico, Guatemala)
....

QQ Quick quiz on letter-number grid references

Use the map of Jamaica on **pages 26 and 27** of your *Caribbean School Atlas* and write in the number-letter for the grid square where the following places are located.

1 The highest point in the island ....

2 Wait-A-Bit in the Cockpit Country..............

3 Jamaica's most easterly point (Morant Point)
....

4 Jamaica's most southerly point (Portland Point) ....

5 The tourism capital of the west, Negril
....

4 Finding the position of a place by its coordinates

 NEW SKILL

Know that cartographers have drawn imaginary lines encircling the Earth in easterly–westerly and northerly–southerly directions, lines of latitude and longitude respectively. Be able to pinpoint places by stating the crossing point of latitude and longitude lines.

Why are degrees used to state position?

Earth is a sphere. If you look down at the Earth from space, it looks like a circle. Your teacher will have a **globe**, which is a model of planet Earth, and can show you.

In mathematics, a circle measured from its centre is 360 degrees. The symbol for degree is °. Therefore, to state positions on the surface of the sphere we call Earth, map-makers draw imaginary circles which cross each other at right angles.

On the globe, circles are drawn parallel to one another between the **North Pole** and the **South Pole**. The longest of the east-west circles is called the **Equator**. The circles parallel to the Equator are called lines of latitude. At the North Pole and the South Pole, latitude is a point.

Another set of circles is drawn at right angles to lines of latitude around the sphere Earth; these lines pass through the North and the South Poles. We call these lines of longitude.

Let's see why these lines are numbered in degrees. The two diagrams explain.

The first diagram shows that lines of latitude are based on an imaginary point in the centre of the Earth. The Equator, the longest east-west line, is called zero degrees, 0°.

The North Pole is a point at 90°N. All the lines between the Equator and the North Pole are lines of latitude north of the Equator. For example, you can see Jamaica on the diagram between the 15°N line and the 30°N line. Jamaica is near the 18°N line. 18° cannot be shown on this small diagram.

The South Pole is a point at 90°S. All the lines between the Equator and the South Pole are lines of latitude south of the Equator. For example, you can see that the city of Cape Town, in South Africa, marked on the diagram, is between the 30°S line and the 45°S line. Cape Town is near the 34°S line of latitude.

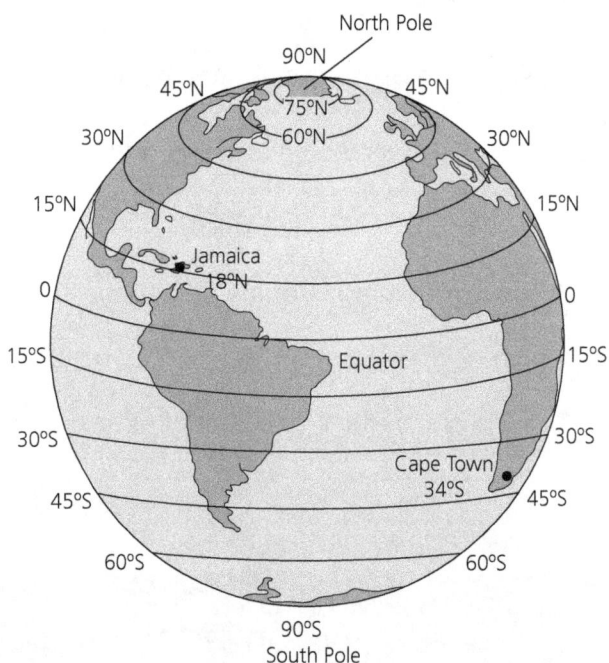

Lines of latitude numbered in degrees

At right angles to lines of latitude are lines of longitude. The next diagram shows you that if you look down at Earth from above the Equator, you would see another circle of 360°.

4 Finding the position of a place by its coordinates

Lines of longitude join the North and South poles at one-degree intervals – the small diagram below can only show lines that are 15° apart. These lines are numbered east and west of the Greenwich Meridian, which is explained on page 12. The lines meet on the far side of Earth from Greenwich, at 180°.

Lines of longitude are therefore numbered east and west of the Greenwich Meridian. On the diagram below, you can see the lines numbered 15°E, 30°E and so on to the east of 0°. And you can see 15°W, 30°W and so on to the west of the Greenwich Meridian.

Guyana is marked on the diagram. The 60°W line of longitude runs through Guyana. Now find Addis Ababa in Ethiopia, which is marked on the diagram and is east of the Greenwich Meridian. You will see that it lies between 30°E and 45°E. This city lies near the line of longitude 39°E.

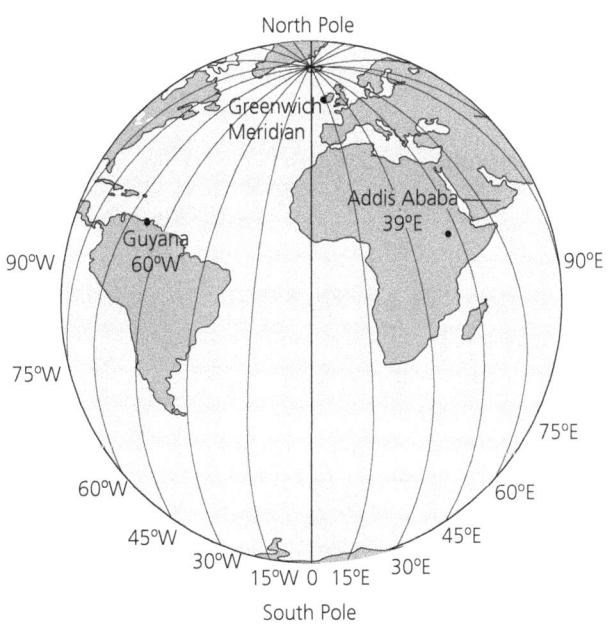

Lines of longitude numbered in degrees

You may know, from mathematics, that a degree is divided into 60 minutes (60'). And a minute comprises 60 seconds (60"). We can therefore be precise about the latitude and longitude of a place by stating it according to degrees, minutes and seconds.

On some of the maps in your *Caribbean School Atlas* you will find that lines of latitude and longitude are given in degrees and minutes. Look for example at the map of Grenada on **page 44**. Look for the line of latitude 12 degrees 10 minutes (12°10'). You can also see degrees and minutes on the map of Trinidad on **page 48**. See how quickly you can find three more maps in the Caribbean Countries section of the atlas that show degrees and minutes.

> Now answer the following questions about degrees and minutes.
>
> 1 What is the line of latitude (degrees and minutes) that passes through Nevis Peak? (**page 39**) .... degrees .... minutes
>
> 2 Which line of latitude passes through the town Four Cross Roads in Saint John parish, Barbados? (**page 46**) .... degrees .... minutes
>
> 3 Using the same map of Barbados, name the line of longitude that passes through the international airport in Christchurch parish: .... degrees .... minutes
>
> 4 What is the line of longitude that passes through the town of Old Road in Antigua? (**page 38**) .... degrees .... minutes
>
> 5 Trinidad's famous Pitch Lake near Brighton in Siparia (**page 48**) is a little south of latitude .... degrees .... minutes

Practice with lines of latitude

As explained above, imaginary lines of latitude circle the Earth in an easterly-westerly direction. The circle around the centre of the Earth is called the Equator. It is zero degrees (0°) of latitude. The following diagram is a simplified one.

Lines of latitude to the north of the Equator are so many degrees north (°N). Look for the 20°N line and the 60°N line on the world map on atlas **pages 56 and 57**. The map does not have the N after the number of degrees, but you should always write in the letter N for north or S for south when you write down a line of latitude.

PART 1 MAP SKILLS

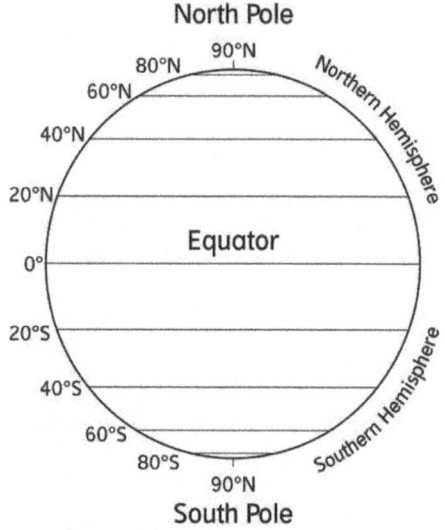

Lines of latitude

The longitude line zero degrees (0°) passes through Greenwich in London, England. This is called the **Prime Meridian** (or the Greenwich Meridian). On the opposite side of the world, 180° passes through the Pacific Ocean (see atlas **page 57**).

Going west from the Prime Meridian, lines of longitude are numbered in degrees west (for example: 20°W, 100°W, 150°W).

Going east from the Prime Meridian, lines are numbered in degrees east (for example: 30°E).

Look at the simplified diagram below, showing one half of the world. The lines to the west of the Prime Meridian meet with the lines to the east at 180° (which is therefore neither east nor west).

The letters E (for east) or W (for west) are not put by the number of degrees on the atlas map (space does not permit). But you must always write the letter °E or °W when you write your answers in this workbook.

Using the world maps on atlas **pages 56 to 59**, which line of latitude is shown going through:

6 Cuba ....

7 Japan ....

8 Bay of Bengal ....

9 Arabia ....

10 Portugal ....

These lines are all north of the Equator. Did you remember to put °N after the numbers?

A line of latitude to the south of the Equator is so many degrees south (°S). Using the maps on atlas **page 71**, find a line of latitude that goes through:

11 New Zealand's North Island ....

12 Solomon Islands ....

13 Australia's Northern Territory ....

14 Port Morseby, capital of Papua New Guinea ....

Did you remember to write in °S to the right of every answer?

Practice with lines of longitude

As you learned above, imaginary lines of longitude join the North Pole and the South Pole in a northerly-southerly direction.

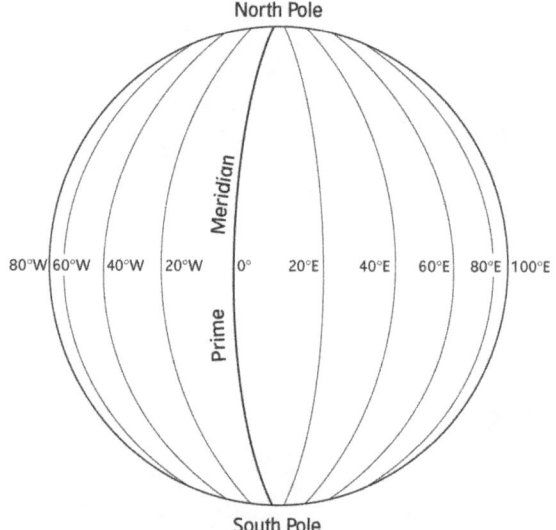

Lines of longitude

Look on the world maps on atlas **pages 56 to 59** to find which line of longitude goes through:

15 Falkland Islands ....

16 Ecuador ....

17 Thailand ....

18 Turkmenistan ....

19 The Ethiopian Highlands ....

Did you remember to write in °E or °W?

4 Finding the position of a place by its coordinates

Practice using latitude and longitude lines together

Every place on the Earth's surface has a different latitude-longitude **coordinate**. We can state its position by the point of intersection between one line of latitude and one line of longitude.

The diagram below shows points where lines cross or intersect. On atlas **page 64** you can see the ocean where 0° latitude crosses 0° longitude. The point of intersection is in the Gulf of Guinea.

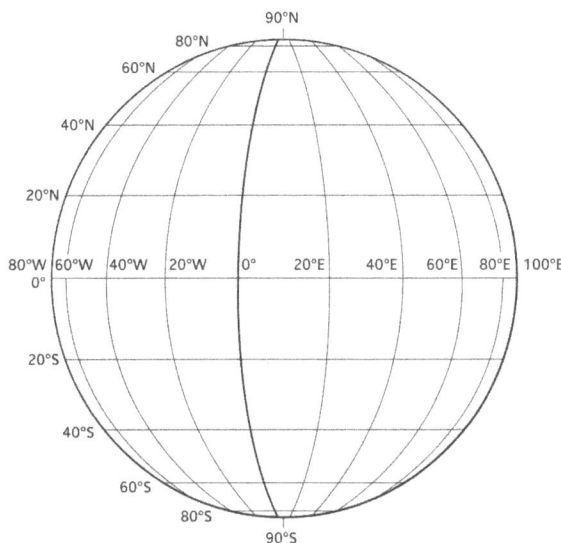

Lines of latitude and longitude

Now look at the map of the Caribbean on atlas **pages 10 and 11**. Can you find the place where 20°N crosses 75°W? It is Guantanamo Bay, part of Cuba controlled by the USA. These lines are all north of the Equator. We say that Guantanamo Bay is at 20°N 75°W.

Latitude is always stated before longitude. So that you don't forget, remember that in the alphabet, A (the second letter of the word latitude) comes before O (the second letter of the word longitude).

Look at the lines of latitude and longitude shown on the map on atlas **pages 8 and 9**. Complete the following sentences.

20 The Caribbean Sea is between lines of latitude .... and ....

21 The Caribbean Sea is between lines of longitude .... and ....

Now turn to the map of the Caribbean on atlas **pages 10 and 11**. Which country is found at each of the following coordinates?

22 10°N 85°W ....

23 10°N 75°W ....

24 5°N 60°W ....

25 25°N 78°W ....

26 List the three countries crossed by longitude 85°W ....
....

Use the atlas pages given in the following questions to find the approximate latitude and longitude coordinates of these towns. Use the nearest line to each place given on the maps in stating your answer.

27 Spanish Town, Jamaica
(page 27) ....

28 Castries, St Lucia
(page 42) ....

29 La Romain, Trinidad
(page 48) ....

30 Loubiere, Dominica
(page 41) ....

QQ Quick quiz on latitude–longitude coordinates

Use the map of Trinidad and Tobago on **page 48** of your *Caribbean School Atlas* and tick the correct answer.

1 The region found where latitude 10°15'N crosses longitude 61°15'W is:
   a Princes Town
   b Sangre Grande
   c Siparia
   d Diego Martin

2 Trinidad's highest point, Mount Aripo, is close to:
   a 61°15'N 10°45'W
   b 61°15'S 10°45'W
   c 10°45'E 61°30'S
   d 10°45'W 61°15'N

PART I MAP SKILLS

3. The island of Little Tobago, east of Tobago, lies on the following line of longitude:
   a 60°30'N ☐   c 60°30'E ☐
   b 60°30'S ☐   d 60°30'W ☐

4. Trinidad's north to south highway from San Juan to San Fernando follows the following line of longitude:
   a 61°32'W ☐   c 61°28'W ☐
   b 61°32'E ☐   d 61°28'E ☐

5. Land in Trinidad where latitude 10°15' crosses longitude 61°15' is:
   a 0–100 m high ☐
   b 100–200 m high ☐
   c 200–400 m high ☐
   d 400–1,000 m high ☐

5 Reading symbols on maps

 NEW SKILL

Practise using the key of a map and make sense of what a map is showing through symbols. Recognise that symbols may be shapes, lines, colours, numbers or letters. Know that sometimes words may be abbreviated on a map if there is not enough room for the complete word. Note: you will learn to interpret colour tints – used to show height of the land – in the next chapter.

Pictures and drawings cannot be used to show where things are on a map – there would not be enough room to show everything!

In any case, pictures and drawings cannot show some things. For example, it would be difficult to tell if a place is a capital city, an important town or a small town just by looking at a picture. There has to be a way to show what kind of settlement it is.

When a map is made, the cartographer selects the most important things to show for the area covered by the map. Symbols are used to show the things the cartographer selected.

Symbols are points or lines or colours. Some points are shapes that you can recognise. Sometimes a point is marked by a letter or number or both. Each symbol has a special meaning. Every map in your atlas has a key to unlock the meaning of each symbol. The key explains what each symbol represents.

> Look at the white box to the right of the map of St Kitts and Nevis on atlas **page 39**. How many symbols are shown in this key? (When counting, include the point symbols, the line symbols and the colour symbols used to represent the height of the land.)
>
> ....
>
> Did you get the same total as your friends?

> Let's find examples of each type of symbol. After you have found examples, we will look at each kind of symbol one by one. We can use the physical and political maps of the world on **pages 56 to 57 and 58 to 59**. Work in a small group to find two examples of each of the following kinds of symbol.
> - Point symbols used to show a country's capital city and its large towns.
> - Point symbols used to show the summit of large mountains.
> - Point numbers used to show the hottest and coldest places in each continent.
> - Lines used for rivers and international boundaries.
> - Colours used to show the height of the land and the depth of the ocean.

5 Reading symbols on maps

Point symbols

On a map, each symbol has a specific meaning. But the same symbol may have another meaning on a different map. Therefore, the rule is: always check the meaning of a symbol in the key of the map you are using.

Sometimes a point symbol, such as a mountain peak, will have a number beside it. If the point is a peak, the number will tell you how high it is above sea level.

⏰ Let's link symbols used in the Caribbean Countries section of your *Caribbean School Atlas* with the correct meaning. You will find these symbols used across **pages 23 to 55**. One example has been done for you – the symbol used to show an important airport. Now draw lines linking the other symbols with the correct meaning.

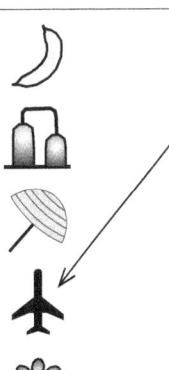

tourism area
garment manufacture
airport
mangrove
banana growing
rum distillery
oilfield
botanic garden
watersports

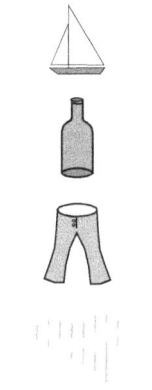

⏰ Look at the atlas map of the world on **pages 56 and 57**. Letters and numbers are used to help you find points of special interest. For example, all the places beginning with the letter K show the point that is highest in each continent. There is a letter K together with a number for each continent. Quickly find the highest point in Asia. What is its name? How high is it in metres? You should have answered 8,850 metres.

Now answer the following questions about points across the world shown on **pages 56 and 57**.

1 In which country is the coldest place in North America? ....

2 In which country is the wettest place in Europe? ....

3 Which is the driest city in Asia? ....

4 Which river is Africa's longest? ....

5 Which island is Africa's biggest? ....

Line symbols

When features follow a line across a landscape, such as a road, a river, a railway or a boundary, line symbols are used to show the position and direction of the feature. Look at the map of Belize on atlas **page 23**. With your finger, follow the path of the line symbol used to show:
- the New River in Orange Walk district
- the road linking Belmopan and Belize City
- the boundary between Belize and Guatemala
- the boundary that separates Stann Creek district from Belize's other districts
- the line of coral reefs around Turneffe Island.

⏰ Now look at the map of Barbados on atlas **page 46** and answer the following questions about the use of line symbols on this topographic map:

6 What kind of road joins the airport to Black Rock, shown as a white line? ....

7 What kind of road links Black Rock to Holetown to its north? ....

8 What line symbol is used to show parish boundaries? ....

9 Do all the rivers in St Philip parish flow into the sea? ....

10 Which one of the following coastlines of Barbados has no coral reefs? South-east, south, west or north-east? ....

Colour tints on political maps

Political maps show the countries of a continent, or the administrative areas, such as parishes or districts, within a country. In political maps, colours are used to distinguish one country, or one area, from another. These colours have no meaning and are not shown in a key.

Look, for example, on the Caribbean map on atlas **pages 10 and 11**. Jamaica and Colombia are both shown in orange. But this does not indicate any similarity between these two countries. Colours used in political maps are randomly selected.

Symbols used for water features

Blue symbols are used on physical maps in atlas maps for water features: rivers, canals, lakes, seas, oceans. A river is shown by a blue line. Only the most important rivers are named in your atlas. A canal is also shown by a blue line; canals are human-made so are straighter than rivers. Lakes and dams are tinted blue like the sea.

If a river is seasonal (which means that it dries out in the dry season) it is shown by a broken blue line. Look at the parish of St Philip in Barbados on atlas **page 46**. You will see several broken blue lines in that parish. Now see if you can find some seasonal rivers in the southern part of Jamaica's Clarendon parish on atlas **pages 26–27**.

The source of a river is always higher than its mouth. In the Caribbean, most rivers rise at a spring (the source), and flow downwards to the sea (the mouth of the river).

For example, the source of the northern Oropuche river in Trinidad (**page 48**) is near Mount Aripo, in the Northern Range. It flows southwards down the hills, then eastwards to its mouth in a swampy area and empties into Matura Bay. Follow its path with your finger!

Now look at the map of Dominica (atlas **page 41**) and complete the following sentences.

11 The Belle Fille river rises near the mountain called .... and enters the sea just south of the town of ....

12 The source of the .... river is near the Morne Diablotins and enters the sea near Glanvillia to the south of Portsmouth.

13 The Roseau river rises near .... and flows through the capital of Dominica named .... before flowing into the sea.

Abbreviations

Abbreviations are used on maps if space does not allow for an entire word to be printed. Abbreviations are not symbols. Look on the world map on atlas **page 59**, for example, and you will see three countries labelled EST, LAT and LITH. These are abbreviations of the country names. Now look on the map of Europe on **page 67**. You will find that these three countries are Estonia (EST), Latvia (LAT) and Lithuania (LITH).

Look at **page 59** again. Can you find five country names abbreviated to SLOV, HUNG, CR, B-H and MONT? Now look at **page 67** and write in the full names of these countries.

14 SLOV is ....

15 HUNG is ....

16 CR is ....

17 B-H is ....

18 MONT is ....

5 Reading symbols on maps   23

Practice in interpreting symbols

Point symbols

What is represented by each of these symbols in the atlas?

19 🐄 (brown; page 51) ....

20 ■ (red; page 48) ....

21 🌳 (green; page 53) ....

22 ⛳ (green; page 53) ....

23 🏭 (red; page 55) ....

24 ⛰ (grey; page 54) ....

25 ● (red; page 54) ....

26 🚢 (blue; page 52) ....

27 (blue; page 52) ....

28 ✓ (green; page 51) ....

29 ◇ (yellow; page 55) ....

30 (black; page 53) ....

These questions will help you get used to using a map's key. You will find each number beside a point symbol. Use the key to find out what the following numbers mean.

31 The number 605 in the purple ship symbol for Antigua and Barbuda on page 21. ....

32 The number 985 beside a black triangle in the middle of Nevis on page 39. ....

33 The number 9 in a red circle in Trinidad's Northern Range (page 53). ....

34 The number 8850 in the Himalayas mountains on page 68. ....

35 The number 2010 beside a red dot over Haiti on page 81. ....

Line symbols

For the following atlas pages, explain what the red line symbol means by using the key. Remember that each atlas map has its own key showing the meaning of its symbols.

36 Page 8: red line joining Havana and Santiago in Cuba.
....

37 Page 12: red line with arrowhead on the top map of the Caribbean.
....

38 Page 13, top map: red line with word Jeanne.
....

39 Page 14, top map: red line linking Santiago in Cuba with Puerto de Santa Gloria in Jamaica.
....

40 Page 32, Resources map: red lines linking Discovery Bay and Ocho Rios with bauxite mining areas to the south.
....

41 Page 52, Resources map: red line joining offshore gas fields with Port Lisas.
....

42 Page 81, top map: red lines on the map.
....

PART 1 MAP SKILLS

Colour tints

What is the colour red used to show on:

43 Page 4, top three diagrams ....

44 Page 21 ....

45 Page 30, top map ....

46 Page 79 ....

47 Page 85, top map ....

Symbols for water features

Look at the Caribbean maps in your atlas for answers to the following questions.

48 What is the name of the river that marks Guyana's boundary with Suriname? (page 54) ....

49 What is the name of the river in Trinidad that enters the Gulf of Paria just south of Port of Spain? (page 48) ....

50 Name the lake near the summit of St Vincent's La Soufrière (page 43) ....

51 Which island on page 38 has no river at all? ....

52 What is the product of the Witte Pan area in the south of Bonaire (page 45)? ....

53 What name is given to the kind of waterway constructed by humans rather than by nature? (Look at the map of Panama on page 8 for an example.) ....

54 What is a lake called when it is open to the sea by a small channel? (Look on the Barbuda map on page 38.) ....

Some symbols are not explained in the key because the cartographer thinks you can easily work out their meaning. Here are some examples. What does each of the following lines represent?

55 Page 4, middle diagram at top of the page: thick black line in the plan of a room ....

56 Page 11: purple line around the pink area labelled Guyana ....

57 Page 28: blue tiny lines on the maps of Jamaican parishes ....

Practice with symbols

Use your skill with symbols to make a map of your journey from home to school. Use all five types of symbol referred to above – lines for roads and rivers, tints for forests or farmland or urban areas you pass through, points for bus stops perhaps, shapes to show interesting places on the way, such as a police station, and numbers to show points of interest.

key

6 Interpreting landscape

Quick quiz on symbols used on maps

Questions 1 to 9 show symbols used in your *Caribbean School Atlas*. In this workbook, they are printed in black; in the atlas they are various colours. In the table, write what the symbol represents on maps on the given page, and say whether it is a line, shape, tint or number symbol.

Question	1	2	3	4	5	6	7	8	9
Symbol used in your atlas	✈	▭	───	⛩	⑨	◗	←	■	—
Its colour in your atlas	black	grey	red	black	pink	green	pink	red	purple
You can find it on this page of your atlas	10	31	34	40	47	52	55	65	69
What does it represent?									
Which of the following kinds of symbol is it: line, shape, tint or number?									

6 Interpreting landscape

🔒 NEW SKILL

Acquire skill in interpreting the colour tints used on physical maps to indicate the height of the land – or the depth of the ocean. By interpreting landscape, you will better understand patterns, both natural and human-made.

Your *Caribbean School Atlas* has a topographical map for every Caribbean country. As explained earlier, a topographical map shows aspects of both the physical and the human-made landscape. The focus of this chapter is on how colour tints are used to show the physical landscape – how high the land is and whether it is flat, gently sloping or mountainous.

We are using the term physical map in this workbook, but other terms with the similar meanings are landscape map and relief map.

Colour tinting to show elevation

Look at the map of St Kitts and Nevis at the top of atlas page 39. You will see a key to the right of the map, which explains the meaning of the colour tints used. How many colour tints are used on this map to show the height of the land above sea level? Your response should be five! You should notice that each tint shows a range of height, such as between 400 and 1,000 metres above sea level.

Starting from sea level, green denotes the lowest land, between 0 and 100 metres above sea level. As the land gets higher, the tint changes – first to pale green, then brownish yellow, then pale brown and finally a reddish-brown. The reddish-brown tint shows land in St Kitts that is over 1,000 metres high. This is in just one area, around Mount Liamuiga. There is no land in Nevis above 1,000 metres. Can you find the highest point in Nevis? What is its elevation?

Sometimes land is below the level of the sea. The key shows that a grey-green tint is used for such areas. Can you find any land in St Kitts or Nevis that is below sea level?

PART 1 MAP SKILLS

⏰ A blank copy of the scale is given here. Use your colour pencils to copy the five tints for the St Kitts and Nevis map for land higher than sea level. Write in what each colour means in terms of the range of height for land tinted with each tint.

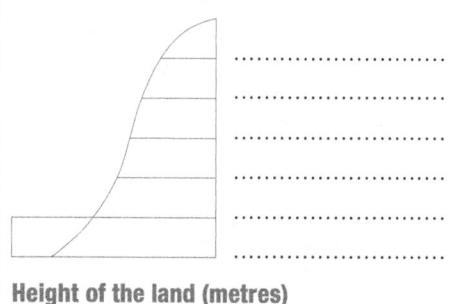

Height of the land (metres)

⏰ Look at the colours used to show topography on the map of Jamaica (**pages 26 and 27**). The key tells you what each colour tint represents. It is different from the key for the St Kitts and Nevis map. Use the colour tint to find out the height above sea level of the following Jamaican places.

1. Christiana in Manchester (E3) is between .... and .... metres above sea level.

2. The Blue Mountains between Portland and St Andrew (H3) are over .... metres above sea level.

3. Clarks Town in Trelawny (D2) is between .... and .... metres above sea level.

4. Montego Bay in St James (C2) is between .... and .... metres above sea level.

5. Land to the south of Portmore in St Catherine (G4) is between .... and .... metres above sea level.

Remember! The same colour tint does not mean the same range of height on every topographical map. You must always check the key. Brown on the Jamaica map means land that is over 4,000 metres above sea level. But look at the world map on atlas **pages 56 and 57**. The same brown tint on this map means that the land is over 6,000 metres high.

⏰ Use keys to the following maps in your atlas to find what green (not pale green) colour tinting denotes:

6. Green on the Caribbean topographical map (**page 8**) denotes land between .... and .... metres above sea level.

7. Green on the Belize topographical map (**page 23**) denotes land between .... and .... metres above sea level.

8. Green on the Guyana topographical map (**page 54**) denotes land between .... and .... metres above sea level.

9. Green on the Europe topographical map (**page 66**) denotes land between .... and .... metres above sea level.

Colour tinting to show depth of seas and oceans

Just as land is measured in number of metres above sea level, the depth of the sea is measured in metres below sea level. Look at the world physical map on **pages 56 and 57**. The key gives four shades of blue – light blue for the shallowest waters to deep blue for the deepest.

⏰ Use the world physical map and its key to complete the following sentences.

10. The Caribbean Sea is generally between .... and .... metres deep.

11. The ocean around Bermuda is between .... and .... metres deep.

12. The depth of the ocean around the Mariana Trench in the Pacific Ocean is more than .... metres deep.

Spot height

As well as using colour, topographical maps also show the exact height of selected mountain peaks by a symbol and number. Look for the little black triangle that marks the highest point. The number beside it gives the height. It is called a *spot height*.

> ⏰ Look at the maps of Antigua and Barbuda on atlas page 38. Antigua's highest point is Mount Obama. It is 402 metres above sea level. Barbuda is almost flat. Its highest point is only 39 metres above sea level and is called The Highlands – 39 metres is the height of a ten-storey building.

> ⏰ Use the spot height to find the height of the following mountain peaks in your atlas.
>
> 13 Nevis Peak (page 39) .... metres
>
> 14 Morne Diablotins, Dominica (page 41)
>
> .... metres
>
> 15 Mount Hillaby, Barbados (page 46)
>
> .... metres
>
> 16 Mount Roraima on the boundary
>
> of Guyana and Venezuela (page 54)
>
> .... metres
>
> 17 Mount Everest in the Himalayas
>
> mountains (page 68) .... metres

Patterns affected by topography

Topography influences many human activities, such as:
- where towns and cities are built
- where dams are constructed
- where transportation networks are routed
- where economic activity is feasible.

Let's look at one pattern that is always affected by topography – *road patterns*.

Atlas maps show the main roads of a country. They do not show all the roads – the smaller roads are shown on larger-scale maps. As you found, roads are shown on Caribbean maps in your *Caribbean School Atlas* by red lines.

Where are roads constructed? It is much easier to construct a road on flat land than across hills and mountains. You will find the pattern of roads on a flat island different from that on a hilly island. On flat islands, roads will often fan out in several directions from an important town. On hilly islands, most roads are built on the flatter land around the coast.

> ⏰ Here are two imaginary islands, one flat and one hilly. They have different road patterns. Let us call the road pattern on the flat island Type A, and the pattern on the hilly island Type B.
>
>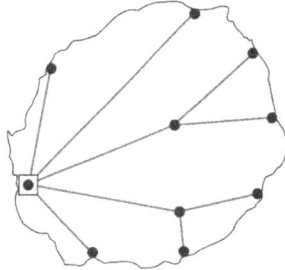
>
> **TYPE A:** Road pattern on a flat island – roads fan out from the main town
>
>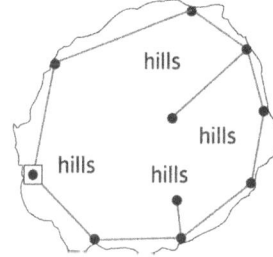
>
> **TYPE B:** Road pattern on a hilly island – roads keep to low-lying land around the coast
>
> Now look at the roads of each of the islands below and identify the pattern as Type A or Type B.
>
> 18 Nevis (page 39) is Type ....
>
> 19 Barbados (page 46) is Type ....
>
> 20 Barbuda (page 38) is Type ....
>
> 21 Antigua (page 38) is Type ....
>
> 22 St Vincent (page 43) is Type ....
>
> 23 St Lucia (page 42) is Type ....

PART 1 MAP SKILLS

Practice on elevation

Use the topographical map of Trinidad and Tobago on atlas **page 48** to respond to the following questions:

24 What is the height of the Siparia region in the south of Trinidad? Between .... and .... metres high.

25 Which is higher: **a** Northern Range of Trinidad or **b** Main Ridge of Tobago? ....

26 How many roads pass through the Northern Range of Trinidad? ....

27 Estimate how much of Trinidad is less than 100 metres above sea level: 100 or 80 or 60 or 40 or 20 per cent? ....

28 Is the road pattern of Tobago affected by the island's Main Ridge? ....

Complete the following table on spot heights. You will have to refer to both the physical and country maps of the continents to fill in the three columns.

Question	Continent	Atlas pages	Country with highest peak	Name of highest peak	Elevation in metres
29	North America	60–61			
30	South America	62–63			
31	Africa	64–65			
32	Europe	66–67			
33	Asia	68–69			
34	Australia and the Pacific	70–71			

QQ Quick quiz on elevation

Select the correct response for these quiz questions on tints, spot heights and road patterns, using the Barbados map on **page 46**. Tick a, b, c or d.

1 The Crane, in the parish of St Philip, is:
   a 0–100 metres above sea level
   b 100–200 metres above sea level
   c 200–400 metres above sea level
   d 400–1,000 metres above sea level

2 Nowhere in Barbados is higher than:
   a 0 m   c 200 m
   b 100 m   d 400 m

3 The peak of Mount Hillaby is:
   a 338 m   c 3,260 m
   b 340 m   d 3,400 m

4 Barbados's airport was constructed:
   a on low-lying flat land
   b on the high land in the centre of the island
   c on land below sea level
   d near the tourist resorts in St James

5 The road pattern of Barbados shows:
   a roads only around the coastline
   b roads avoiding land over 200 metres high
   c roads radiating out from the capital Bridgetown
   d roads only in the south of the island

7 Stating direction

NEW SKILL

Learn the eight principal points of the compass. Practise the skill of stating the direction from one place to another.

Cardinal points of the compass

Look through your *Caribbean School Atlas*. On one map of every place you will find a diagram showing the cardinal directions.

These are sometimes called the principal points of the compass. A compass is an instrument that was used to find direction before the era of smartphones. A compass rose is a symbol on every map to show the direction of north, the North Point.

Look at the letter N on one of these diagrams. It means that the direction from the centre of the diagram along the line to the arrow-point N and beyond is northward. If you continued in a northward direction you would reach the North Pole.

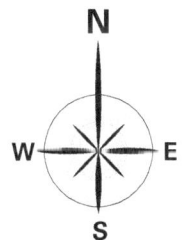

Points of the compass

What is the meaning of letters in the diagram above?

1. N ....
2. S ....
3. E ....
4. W ....

Intermediate directions

Midway between the four principal main directions there are intermediate ones. For example, the direction midway between north and east is north-east (NE). Add these four intermediate points to the diagram.

Write down the meaning of letters for the four intermediate directions between the cardinal points:

5. SE means ....
6. SW means ....
7. NW means ....
8. NE means ....

Complete these sentences (first write two words, then two letters):

9. The direction midway between S and E is called .... or ....
10. The direction midway between S and W is called .... or ....
11. The direction midway between N and W is called .... or ....

What direction is shown by each arrow?

12. ....
13. ....
14. ....
15. ....

Make your own direction finder

To help you work out the direction of one place from another, copy the diagram on the right on a piece of card or paper and cut it out. Make a hole in the middle the size of a small coin. You can call this your direction finder.

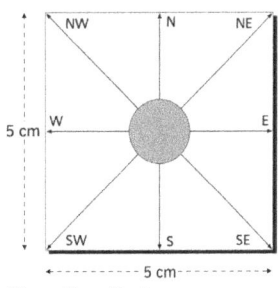

Direction finder

PART I MAP SKILLS

How to use your direction finder, step by step

Step 1. Find two places on the atlas map. For example, what is the direction of Bathsheba in Barbados from Bridgetown? Find both towns on atlas **page 46**.

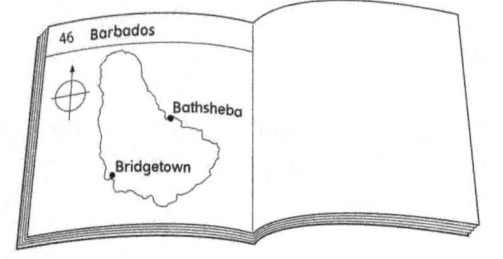

Step 2. You want the direction of a place from Bridgetown. Put the direction finder over the symbol for Bridgetown. Make sure the North on the direction finder is pointing the same way as north on the map's North Point.

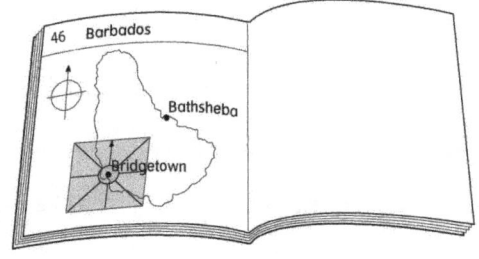

Step 3. Place a ruler with its edge just touching Bridgetown and Bathsheba. The ruler should be on top of the direction finder.

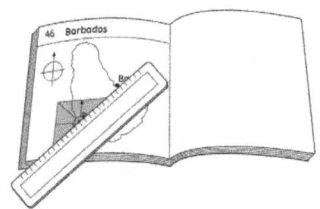

Step 4. Read the direction on your direction finder.

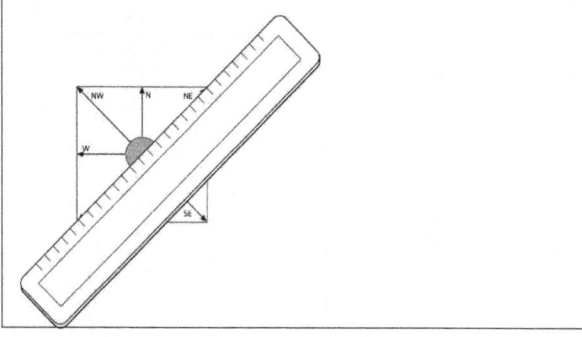

You should have found that Bathsheba is north-east (NE) of Bridgetown.

Practice in stating direction

Look at the map of South America on atlas **page 63**. Use your direction finder and complete these sentences with the correct direction.

16 Guyana is .... of Suriname.

17 Uruguay is .... of Brazil.

18 Manaus is .... of Brasilia.

19 Bogota is .... of Caracas.

20 Asuncion is .... of La Paz.

21 The capitals of two countries, ... and ...., are both due east of the capital of Chile.

Test your classmates on direction! Get into a group of four and complete in the following exercise.
- Each member of the group should select one continent from the maps in the *Caribbean School Atlas* on **pages 60, 61, 64, 65, 66, 67, 68 and 69**. Each student should have a different continent.
- Each student should then make up four questions on directions on the map of his or her continent and write down the answer (kept secret from the other members of the group).
- Then each student should take turns to ask the other members their four questions. The other students should write down their answers.
- By the end of the game, each member of the group will have written answers for three continents: twelve answers in all.
- Finally, share your correct answers with each other.

How many members of your group got all twelve directions correct?

QQ Quick quiz on stating directions

Open your *Caribbean School Atlas* on **pages 8–9**. Use a direction finder to find the correct answers.

1. What direction is the centre of Trinidad from the centre of Tobago? ....
2. Which country is south of Guadeloupe? ....
3. In which direction are the Cayman Islands from the western end of Jamaica? ....
4. What country is found to the west of the Dominican Republic? ....
5. In which direction would you sail from Havana to reach Miami? ....

8 Working out distance by using scale

NEW SKILL

Recognise that every map is drawn to scale. Know that a map's scale may be stated in three different ways. Find the scale of the map you are using. Calculate real distance between two points using scale.

What is scale?

Go to **page 4** of your *Caribbean School Atlas*.

This page explains that a plan of a classroom or a map of a particular area is drawn to **scale**. Neither a plan nor a map can be drawn at the original size – both plan and map must be reduced to fit the size of the space available on the page of the atlas.

The scale drawing of the top of a table is 25 times smaller than the table itself. On the plan, 1 centimetre is equivalent to 25 centimetres of the actual table. This ratio is written as 1:25. You read it or say it as 'one to twenty-five'. This is the scale of the plan.

Now look at the plan of the room to the right of the table-top drawing. Here, 1 centimetre on the plan represents 1 metre of the room. As 1 metre is 100 centimetres, the ratio is 1:100. The next drawing is at 1 centimetre represents 4 metres or 400 centimetres. The ratio is therefore 1:400.

 Look at the three maps in the middle of atlas **page 4** and find the **ratio scale** for each one. Say the ratio scales aloud. Then look at other maps in the atlas and say their ratio scales. For example, if you open your atlas at **pages 8 and 9**, the physical map of the Caribbean region, you would say 'The ratio scale of this map is one to eight million'.

Three ways of stating scale

You have already used two ways of stating scale (1) as a mathematical ratio and (2) as a statement of this ratio in words. There is a third way. This is by transforming the ratio into a drawing called a **scale bar** (also called a linear scale). Look again at atlas **page 4** where a scale bar is shown in the lower right corner of the page.

Scale bars in the *Caribbean School Atlas* show you how many kilometres on the ground are represented by one centimetre on the map.

Look at the scale bar on the map of Montserrat on **page 37**. You will see that 1 centimetre on the topographical map represents 3 kilometres on the ground.

Now look for Montserrat on the Caribbean map on **page 11**. You will find that 1 centimetre on this map represents 80 kilometres. As Montserrat is a mere 16 km from north to south, it is hard to find it on the Caribbean map and no detail about the island is shown.

PART 1 MAP SKILLS

Remember! A map only has one scale. But its scale can be shown in three ways:
- A ratio: the numerator is always 1; the denominator varies from map to map.
- A statement, which explains the ratio in words.
- A scale bar, which converts the ratio into a diagram.

The table shows the three ways of stating scale. Several scales are shown. The tinted spaces have been left blank. Complete the table by filling in the seven tinted spaces.

Ratio scale	Statement of scale	Scale bar
1:8,000,000	1 cm on the map = 80 km on the ground	
1:300,000		Scale 1:300 000 1cm on the map = 3km on the ground 0 3 6 9 12km
	1 cm on the map = 400 km on the ground	Scale 1:40 000 000 This distance is 1500 kilometres
		Scale 1:450 000 1cm on the map = 4.5km on the ground 0 4.5 9 13.5 18km
1:60,000,000		

Larger-scale maps and smaller-scale maps

When you looked at the two maps of Montserrat, the one with detail of hills and roads had a ratio scale of 1:300,000. The one with no detail had a ratio scale of 1:8,000,000.

When the denominator is smaller (300,000 is more than 20 times smaller than 8,000,000) we call this a larger-scale map. The reverse is equally true. The map with a scale of 1:8,000,000 is the smaller-scale map of the two. To fit a map of the entire world on one page (such as atlas **pages 56 and 57**) the scale needs to be 1:100,000,000 or one to one hundred million. We could call such a map a very small-scale map.

1 Write the following ratio scales in order, from the largest scale to the smallest scale:

   a) 1:50,000 b) 1:10,000 c) 1:800,000 d) 1:40,000,000 e) 1:145,000 f) 1:100,000,000
   g) 1:1,000

Largest scale						Smallest scale

2 Find the island of Jamaica on atlas **pages 8, 26, 56, 60 and 61**. Write the five ratio scales of these maps in the boxes, in order from the smallest scale to the largest scale. Be careful copying out ratio scales like these! Make sure you write in the numerator (1) and all the zeros of the denominator.

Smallest scale				Largest scale

8 Working out distance by using scale

Practice stating the scale of a map

Find the ratio scales of the following maps in your *Caribbean School Atlas*.

3 Belize: topography (page 23) scale ....

4 Cuba: topography (page 34) scale ....

5 Trinidad: topography (page 48) scale ....

6 Tobago: topography (page 48) scale ....

7 South America: physical (page 62) scale ....

8 South America: countries (page 63) scale ....

Which of the scales you wrote down in answer to questions 3 to 8 is:

9 The largest scale? ....

10 The smallest scale? ....

Look at Tobago on the two landscape maps on pages 9 and 48 and complete these sentences:

11 The scale of the Tobago map on page 9 is .... and on page 48 is ....

12 The map on page .... is the smaller-scale map.

13 Which map gives more detail on Tobago? smaller scale ☐ larger scale ☐

Use the Glossary to complete the meaning of the following terms:

14 *scale* The .... between a line on a map and the distance on the ground, expressed as a ratio scale or line scale.

15 *large-scale map* A relatively .... area shown at a scale which allows detail.

16 *small scale* A map of a .... area at a scale that does not allow detail to be shown.

17 *scale bar* The scale of a map shown by a .... line and equivalent distances.

How to calculate distance between two points

A scale bar is used to find the distance from one point to another on a map. Let's work out, step by step, how far it is from San Juan (capital of Puerto Rico) to Santo Domingo (capital of the Dominican Republic). Here is the scale bar from page 11 of the *Caribbean School Atlas*.

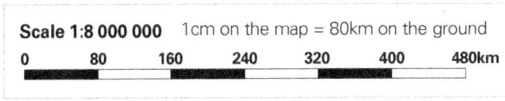

Scale bar for Caribbean Countries map

Use the straight edge of a sheet of paper. Place it on the map, touching the symbols for both cities. Make a mark on the paper by Santo Domingo and by San Juan.

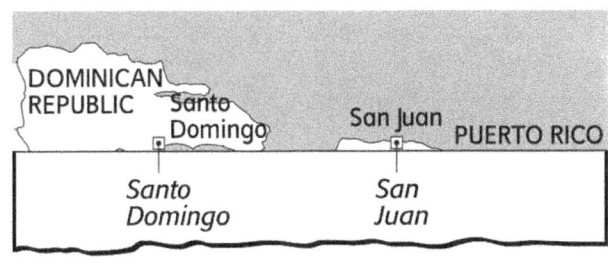

Marking the two points

PART 1 MAP SKILLS

Place the paper against the scale bar. Put the Santo Domingo mark beside 0. You will see the San Juan mark beside 400. The distance between the two cities is 400 kilometres (400 km).

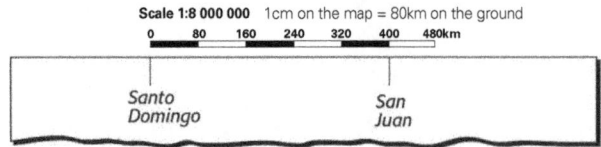

Working out the actual distance

How far is it from Port of Spain (Trinidad) to Georgetown (Guyana)? Work it out. When you place your sheet of paper against the scale bar, you will find that it is too short to read the distance in one go. The distance is more than 480 kilometres. What you must do is mark off the first 500 kilometres on your paper, and measure what is left over. Do you have 100 kilometres extra? Correct. The answer is 500 kilometres plus 100 kilometres. Georgetown is 600 kilometres from Port of Spain.

Some maps do not provide a scale bar but provide a ratio scale or a written statement. You can measure distance between two points using the ratio or the written statement, but these are more complicated. Read the lower half of **page 6** of your atlas for guidance on using these other methods.

Practice estimating distance

> Now find some distances on other maps. Make sure to use the correct scale bar for each map!

18 How far is it from Belmopan to Belize City? (page 23) .... kilometres

19 What is the distance from the border town of Chetumal, in the north of Belize, to the country's south-west point (page 23)? .... kilometres

20 How far is it from Negril, Jamaica, to Morant Point, west to east? (pages 26–27) .... kilometres

21 How wide is Nevis from east to west along latitude line 17°10'? (page 39) .... kilometres

22 How far is Speightstown from Bridgetown, Barbados? (page 46) .... kilometres

23 How far is Trinidad from Venezuela? (Measure from Chacachacare Island's western tip to Patos Island's eastern tip.) (page 48) .... kilometres

24 How far, approximately, is Jamaica from the southern tip of Africa? (pages 58–59) .... kilometres

QQ Quick quiz on calculating distance

Using atlas **pages 8–9** find the distance between the following places.

1 Kingston (Jamaica) and Port-au-Prince (Haiti) .... kilometres

2 Nassau (the Bahamas) and Miami (USA) .... kilometres

3 Havana (Cuba) and Belmopan (Belize) .... kilometres

4 San Juan (Puerto Rico) and Georgetown (Guyana) .... kilometres

9 GAME BOX: MAP SKILLS

 SKILLS PRACTICE

Try these four activities and have fun practising the skills you have acquired. The games cover: map reading, map making, following directions and stating coordinates.

Make a map of your trip plan

You are planning a journey from one town to another. Which way should you travel? Which places will you pass through during your journey?

Imagine you live in **Kingston**. Your father will drive you on a day trip to **Oracabessa** in St Mary to visit your grandmother who is not at all well. On the way there you want to stop in **Spanish Town** to visit its cathedral, which you have heard is one of the oldest in the Americas.

You also want to visit Bob Marley's birthplace near **Claremont** and Marcus Garvey's birthplace of **St Ann's Bay**.

After spending some time with your grandmother, you want to stop at the coastal village of **Boston Bay** in the parish of Portland where the jerking of pork and chicken began in the 1960s, a method of barbecuing meat which has spread across Jamaica and the world. You hope to taste the original jerked pork! You will then head back to Kingston via **Port Morant** in St Thomas before nightfall.

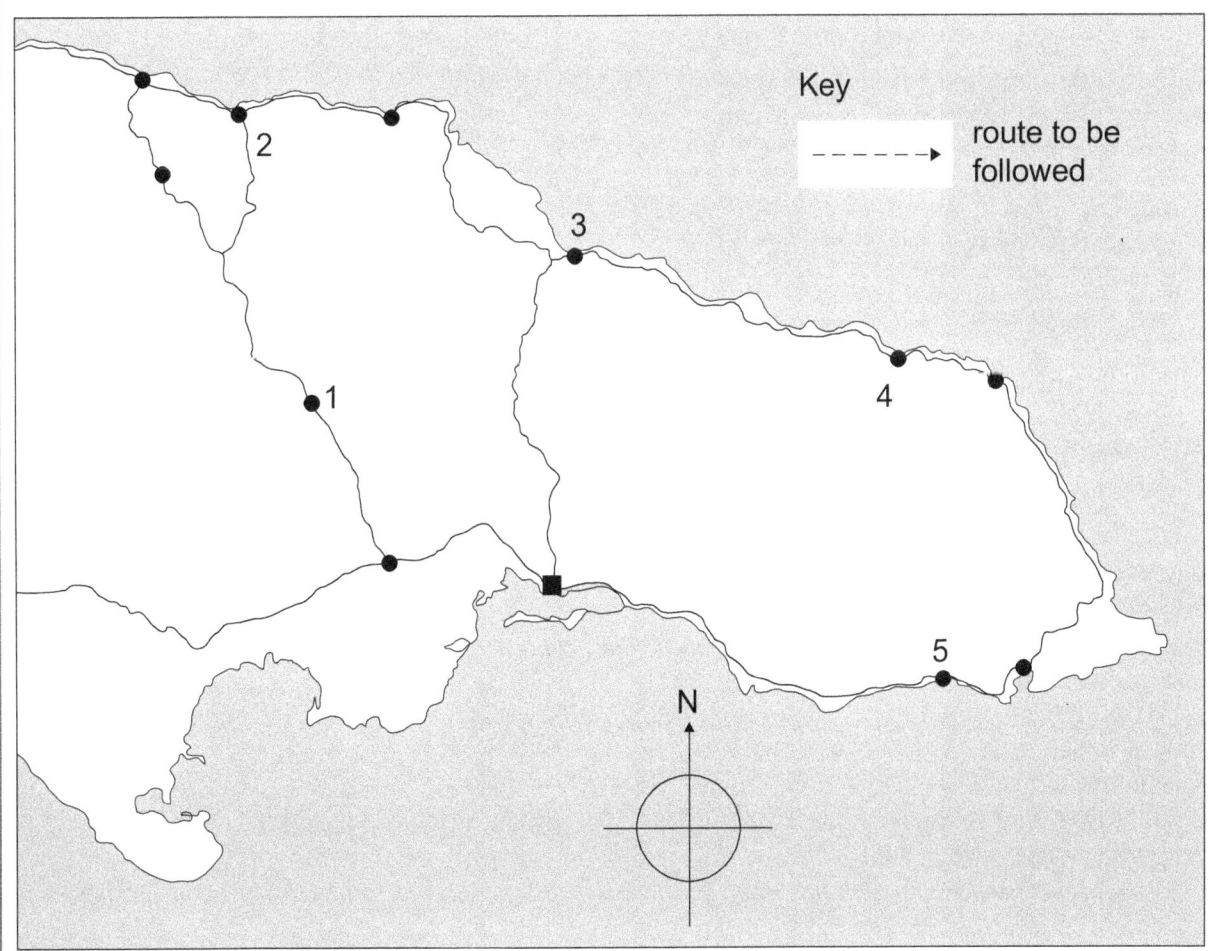

Jamaica: eastern part of the island

CARIBBEAN SCHOOL ATLAS
SKILLS WORKBOOK

This is your task:
- Find the seven places named above on your atlas map of Jamaica (page 27).
- Name them on the sketch map.
- Mark the route you will take on the map. Make sure the key matches the colour you use to mark the route.
- Why did you choose this route?
- Other important towns that you will pass through on your journey are numbered 1 to 5 on the sketch map (**Linstead, Ocho Rios, Annotto Bay, Port Antonio, Morant Bay**).

- Find these towns and write their names beside the correct number:

1 ....

2 ....

3 ....

4 ....

5 ....

Make your own physical map

Make your own physical map of an island by carefully shading the different layers with the correct colours!

Use the outline map of Trinidad on the right. You need four coloured pencils: blue, green, yellow and brown. You will need five tints – you can use the green pencil very lightly to make light green.

This is your task:
- Use the topographical map of Trinidad on atlas **page 48** as a guide.
- Shade the sea pale blue.
- Fill in numbers in the key and shade the five boxes with a colour tint like the atlas map.
- Shade the different layers of the outline map of Trinidad.
- Give your map a title.

The colours show the height of the land above sea level

☐ Over .... metres
☐ .... metres
☐ .... metres
☐ .... metres
☐ .... metres

Name the mountain

Imagine you are making a journey in Dominica. Look at the topographical map on atlas **page 41**. Follow the directions to find out where to go. Each direction tells you which way to turn at a road junction.
- Start at Castle Bruce (B2) and travel north to the first road junction.
- Then turn south and south-west until you reach the next junction at Point Casse.
- Next turn north-east and follow the road until you reach the boundary of the parishes of St Joseph and St David.
- Then look directly south.
- What is the name of the mountain that towers in front of you?

....

CARIBBEAN SCHOOL ATLAS
SKILLS WORKBOOK
37

Work out latitude–longitude coordinates yourself

Fill in coordinates for the Caribbean place that witnessed each event named in each second column of the table. There is only one correct coordinate for each one. Write your answers in degrees; do not use minutes. The first event has been entered for you.

Year	Event	Atlas page	Location	Latitude and longitude coordinate
1978	Independence proclaimed in the country's capital	41	Roseau, Dominica	15°N 61°W
1872	This city becomes capital in place of Spanish Town	29 & 27		
2017	The boundaries of this protected biodiversity hotspot are announced by the Government	33 & 26		
1995	Half of this island was made uninhabitable when a volcano erupted	37		
1973	A treaty was signed in this country to establish CARICOM	19 & 9		
1884	A Jamaican national hero was born in this parish	30 & 26		
1791	Enslaved Africans rebelled against the French and created the first independent country of the Caribbean	9 & 15		

Assess factors affecting settlement decisions

Your school participates in an international schools partner programme. It encourages students and teachers to share information and ideas as they learn about related topics. Your school and your partner school in New Zealand are both learning about the Taino people who inhabited Jamaica before the arrival of Europeans, and the Maroons who established settlements during the colonial era.

Your task is to create a PowerPoint presentation to be viewed by the class in New Zealand via video call and be prepared to respond to questions the New Zealanders might ask you.

a Decide which maps of Jamaica in Caribbean School Atlas will help you with the information you need. Explain your choices here:

....
....
....
....

b Summarise where in the island the Tainos lived and why, and where the Maroons established their settlements.

....
....

c Make notes for Slides 1 to 5 (see spaces opposite column) on the information you will present to the New Zealand class using five PowerPoint slides.

Slide 1: ....
....
....

Slide 2: ....
....
....

Slide 3: ....
....
....

Slide 4: ....
....
....

Slide 5: ....
....

CARIBBEAN SCHOOL ATLAS
SKILLS WORKBOOK

d Suppose one of the New Zealand students asks why Tainos and Maroons settled in the places they did. What reasons would you give to explain the location of Taino settlements?

i ……………………………………………………

ii ……………………………………………………

What reasons would you give to explain the location of Maroon settlements?

i ……………………………………………………

ii ……………………………………………………

Make a map of the village of Petite Ville

In the space provided, create a map using the scale 1 centimetre is equal to 100 metres, and include:

- A key with appropriate symbols for each feature to be drawn on the map
- A main road 1000 metres long from north to south
- Houses on either side of the road
- A playing field 250 metres long and 200 metres wide to the east of the main road
- A small farm that is 300 metres long and 100 metres wide to the south-west
- A compass rose
- A scale bar/linear scale
- A title.
- A Key.

Key

10 Map skills test

Use your *Caribbean School Atlas* to find the correct answer. Only one of the four possible answers given is correct. Tick either A, B, C or D.

SKILLS ASSESSMENT

This test checks map skills you acquired in Chapters 1 to 9.

1 There is a relief map of North America on atlas page:

A 40 ☐   B 50 ☐   C 60 ☐   D 70 ☐

2 Belize River is shown on a map on atlas page:

A 20 ☐   B 23 ☐   C 26 ☐   D 29 ☐

3 Tortola is one of the islands of:

A the Grenadines ☐
B the Bahamas ☐
C the Turks and Caicos Islands ☐
D the British Virgin Islands ☐

4 What is mined where you see a purple triangle on **page 52**?

A Gypsum ☐   C Asphalt ☐
B Oil ☐   D Limestone ☐

10 Map skills test

5 The land shaded yellow on **page 42** is between:
  A 0 and 100 metres above sea level
  B 100 and 200 metres above sea level
  C 200 and 400 metres above sea level
  D 400 and 1,000 metres above sea level

6 Water features north and west of Miami, Florida (**page 8**) are:
  A rivers   C canals
  B lakes   D springs

7 In travelling by road from Kingstown to Barrouallie in St Vincent (**page 43**) you would pass through:
  A Georgetown   C Stubbs
  B Chateaubelair   D Layou

8 The airport in Barbados (**page 46**) is in grid square:
  A C4   C A4
  B B1   D A2

9 What direction is The Quarter from Blowing Point Village in Anguilla (**page 37**)?
  A North-east   C South-west
  B North   D South

10 The direction of Castries from Micoud in St Lucia (**page 42**) is:
  A North-west   C South-west
  B South-east   D North-east

11 Which country is found on the Equator at 100°E (**page 69**)?
  A Bangladesh   C Indonesia
  B China   D Malaysia

12 The location of Mount St Catherine in Grenada (**page 44**) is:
  A 61°40'N 12°10'W
  B 12°10'N 61°40'W
  C 840
  D A2

13 Rainfall over 2,000 millimetres per year in St Vincent (**page 43**) falls:
  A in the west of the island
  B around the capital city
  C in lowland areas
  D in places over 200 metres above sea level

14 The highest mountain in St Lucia (**page 42**) is:
  A Mount Gimie   C Petit Piton
  B Gros Piton   D Mon Renos

15 The scale of the map of Martinique (**page 40**) is:
  A 1:600,000
  B 1:6,000,000
  C 1 centimetre on the map = 12 kilometres on the ground
  D 1,102 square kilometres

16 Which of the following maps on **pages 36 and 37** has the largest scale?
  A Montserrat districts
  B British Virgin Islands topography
  C Anguilla topography
  D Eastern Caribbean islands

17 On **page 41**, the distance from Soufrière to Portsmouth is:
  A 38 kilometres   C 12 kilometres
  B 83 kilometres   D 21 kilometres

18 The distance from London to Athens (**pages 66 to 67**) is:
  A 9,000 kilometres
  B 2,500 kilometres
  C 3,000 kilometres
  D 2,000 kilometres

19 Which is 20 kilometres north-east of San Fernando? (**page 48**)
  A Northern Range
  B Trinity Hills
  C Central Range
  D Montserrat Hills

20 The length of St Lucia (**page 42**) from Pointe du Cap to Cape Moule à Chique is:
  A 40 kilometres
  B 43 kilometres
  C 46 kilometres
  D 49 kilometres

PART 2 INTERPRET DATA, GRAPHS AND PHOTOGRAPHS

11 Interpreting data and diagrams

 **NEW SKILL**

Acquire skills to use and interpret the data in various forms in your *Caribbean School Atlas*.

Forms of data

Information

Everything on every page of the *Caribbean School Atlas* is based on information gathered. Governments, international and local organisations, businesses, universities and individual researchers all gather information. Individual pieces of information are combined to form data. A set of data is information that has been transformed into a form that is convenient for processing and enables interpreting.

> What information does your school collect about you and other students? Get into small groups and think out loud to work out what information the school director and teachers collect about each of you. In your group, make a list of the different kinds of information. Then think how this information is combined so that the school can communicate about its students and its accomplishments. Compare your ideas with those of other groups in your class.

In the first part of this workbook, we looked at how information is displayed through many kinds of map. In this part, we will look at information selected for inclusion in fact files for Caribbean countries and for the six continents. We will then look at how information is displayed in tables and in various kinds of graph.

Fact files

Look at the first page of the atlas section on Caribbean countries – **page 23** shows Belize. In the top right-hand corner, there is a box with information about Belize. We call this a fact file.

BELIZE

Independence 1981
Capital: Belmopan
Area: 22,966 sq km
Population: 388,000 (est.2018)
Languages: English (official), Spanish, Creole, Maya
Sources of national income: sugar, bananas, citrus, fishing, forestry, crude oil, tourism

There is a fact file for each Caribbean country. It shows:
- the national flag
- the year the country became independent
- its capital city
- its area in square kilometres
- an estimate of its total population in 2018
- the languages spoken
- the most important crops and industries.

Tables

A **statistical table** provides information organised according to category. Your *Caribbean School Atlas* has a table of Facts & Figures, **pages 73 to 75**, about every country of the world.

For each continent, countries are listed alphabetically. The first country listed for each continent begins with A, but only for Africa does the last country listed begin with a Z. For every country listed in the table, the columns give its flag, its capital city, its area and its population.

11 Interpreting data and diagrams

Practice using fact files and tables

> This exercise will give you practice in finding information about countries from fact files. You will have to search through all the fact boxes of the Caribbean Countries section (atlas **pages 23 to 55**) to find the answers.

1 In which year did Jamaica and Trinidad and Tobago become independent?

   ....

2 Which Caribbean country became independent in 1978?

   ....

3 Which was the first Caribbean country to win its independence?

   ....

4 Which one of Dominica, Dominican Republic, St Lucia and Montserrat is not a member of the Organisation of Eastern Caribbean States (OECS)?

   ....

5 Which one of Barbados, Guyana, Haiti, and Saba has the largest area?

   ....

6 Which one of the Bahamas, Belize, Dominica and Grenada has the smallest population?

   ....

7 In which one of Cuba, Haiti, Guadeloupe and Martinique is French not the official language?

   ....

8 Which countries do not list tourism as an important industry?

   ....

9 Name two countries where bauxite is mined.

   ....

10 In which English-speaking country is coffee-growing important?

   ....

There are also fact files about the world and its continents. Look through **pages 56 to 70** to see these files of information. To become familiar with what facts are shown, find answers to Questions 11–20. For this exercise you are told the page where the answer is given.

> Write in the correct response for each question.

11 Where is the driest place in Africa and what is its average annual rainfall? (page 56)

   Driest place in Africa ....;

   annual rainfall .... millimetres

12 Which is the largest lake in North America and what is its area? (page 57)

   Lake ....; area ....

13 How many countries in the world have a population of over one hundred million people? (page 58)

   ....

14 What is the population of Nauru, the smallest country in the Pacific? (page 59)

   ....

15 Which country in North America is largest in terms of area? (page 60)

   ....

16 Which of Costa Rica, Cuba, Panama and El Salvador is not a country of Central America? (page 61)

   ....

17 Which is the largest city in South America? (page 62)

   ....

18 Which country of Africa is ranked tenth in terms of area? (page 64)

   ....

19 Which European and Asian countries are largest both in area and population? (pages 66 and 68)

   ....

20 Of the ten largest cities of Asia, how many are in India? (page 69)

   ....

PART 2 INTERPRET DATA, GRAPHS AND PHOTOGRAPHS

> ⏰ Use the Countries Facts & Figures table on **pages 73 to 75** to find the correct response to the following questions:
>
> 21 What is similar about the flags of Algeria, Mauritania, Pakistan and Turkey?
>
> ....
>
> 22 What is similar about the flags of Denmark, Finland, Iceland, Norway and Sweden?
>
> ....
>
> 23 Name the capital of Liberia: ....
>
> 24 Hanoi is the capital of ....
>
> 25 The area of Tuvalu in the Pacific region is .... square kilometres.
>
> 26 The population of Spain is ....
>
> 27 Countries in Asia with a population over one billion (1,000,000,000) are .... and ....
>
> 28 Two countries of Africa that are over two million square kilometres in area are .... and ....

Diagrams

A diagram is a drawing to show the structure or workings of something complex. It shows how something works. A diagram simplifies things by omitting detail. Unlike a map or a graph, it is freely drawn without concern for scale. Your *Caribbean School Atlas* uses diagrams to represent complex events so that you can visualise how things work.

Look at the diagram of a hill on **page 2** of your atlas. The hill is shown three-dimensionally; that is, width and depth/height. It is not related to a real hill. It was drawn to show how the various tints in the key relate to the height of land.

Let's look at the diagram on atlas **page 12** (reproduced below). The maps above the diagram in the atlas are two-dimensional. Together they show how plate boundaries are related to earthquakes, volcanoes and tsunamis. The diagram explains why and how!

This cross-section gives you an idea of what is happening below the surface. The line of section is along 15 degrees North (15°N). Look at this line of latitude on the Caribbean map on **pages 8 and 9**. The line crosses Guatemala and Honduras in the west, passes through the Caribbean Sea, then a little south of Dominica and on to the Atlantic Ocean to the east. The diagram shows the relationship of plate boundaries to volcanic eruptions and earthquakes.
- Is your country affected?

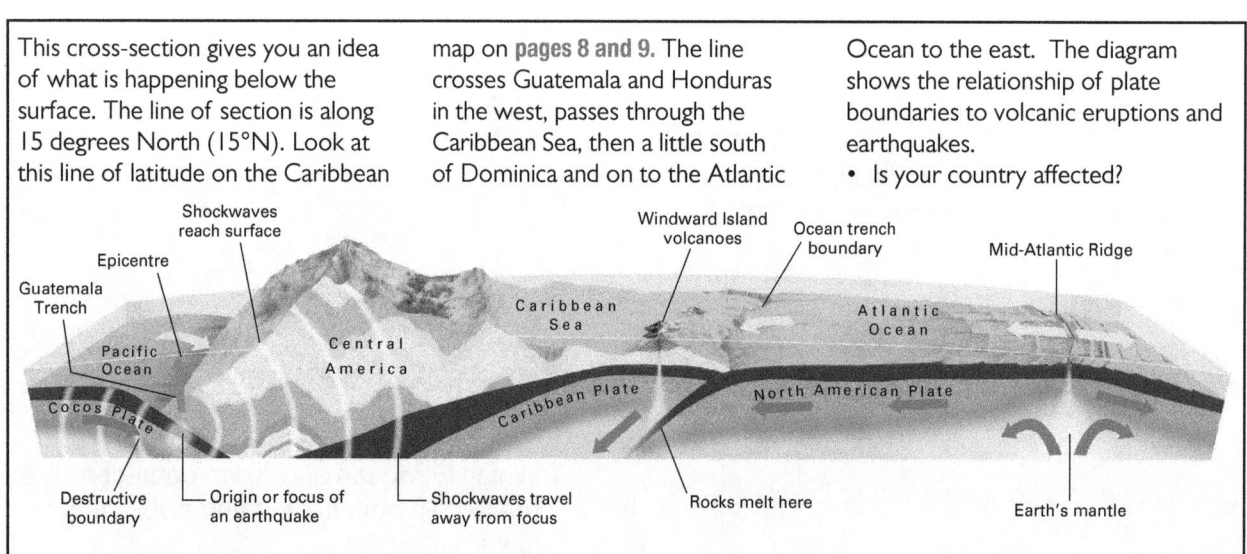

Plate Tectonics in the Caribbean

11 Interpreting data and diagrams

Practice in interpreting diagrams

Find answers to the following questions by looking carefully at the diagram of plate tectonics in the Caribbean on atlas page 12.

29 How many oceans and seas are shown? ....

30 How many plates are shown? ....

31 What happens on the Earth's surface when the North American Plate pushes eastwards against the Caribbean Plate? ....

32 What does the diagram show happening when the Cocos Plate pushes west against the Caribbean Plate? ....

33 From the diagram, what do you think the word 'epicentre' means? ....

Get into a group and discuss what is shown in the diagram of a cross-section through a hurricane at bottom left of atlas page 13. See whether you can relate the diagram to the satellite image of a hurricane to the right of the diagram. Looking at the diagram and image together, discuss the meanings of: vortex, eye, path, dense cloud and landfall.

Look at the diagrams on page 76 and respond to the following questions.

34 What do the white lines depict on the solar system diagram?
....

35 Which of the Sun's planets is nearest to Earth, based on the centre diagram?
....

36 Why does the Moon appear to change shape when we look at it from Earth (see the Moon diagram)?
....

37 How long does it take the planet Neptune to make one complete orbit of the Sun?
....

38 How often would you see a full Moon if you look up to the sky?
....

QQ Quick quiz on interpreting data and diagrams

Select the correct response for these quiz questions about data and diagrams by using your *Caribbean School Atlas*. Tick a, b, c or d.

1 Single pieces of Information can be combined and organised to create:
   a facts ☐
   b data ☐
   c numbers ☐
   d index ☐

2 St Lucia became an independent country in:
   a 1779 ☐
   b 1962 ☐
   c 1971 ☐
   d 1979 ☐

PART 2 INTERPRET DATA, GRAPHS AND PHOTOGRAPHS

3 The diagram at the bottom of **page 77** of your *Caribbean School Atlas* shows that:
   a the tilting of Earth on its axis causes the length of daytime to vary over the course of the year ☐
   b seasons are caused by the tilt of Earth ☐
   c Earth **rotates** on its axis, which is tilted at 66.5° in relation to the Sun ☐
   d days are shortest in Cape Town on 21 December ☐

4 The ten largest cities of South America:
   a all have a population of less than 22 ☐
   b all are north of latitude 10° South ☐
   c all are south of the Equator ☐
   d all have a population of more than 3 million ☐

5 This country is not considered part of Central America:
   a Nicaragua ☐   c Cuba ☐
   b Belize ☐   d Panama ☐

12 Interpreting graphs

 NEW SKILL
Acquire skills to interpret the many types of graph in your *Caribbean School Atlas*.

Types of graph

Line graph

To construct a **line graph**, data is plotted according to the values on the two axes. The dots are joined together into a single line. You can see the dots plotted on the population change graph at the bottom of atlas **page 49**. In the graph to show gas production on **page 52**, the dots are joined together. You can easily see that gas production increased until 2010 and then started falling.

There may be more than one set of data on a line graph so that comparison is easy. Look at the graph on **page 51** comparing the roles of sugar, manufacturing and other contributions to Trinidad and Tobago's economy. This graph has four lines to show four data sets. Which part of the economy has grown fastest?

Pie graph

A **pie graph** is also called a pie chart or a divided circle. The total quantity is represented by a circle. The circle is divided into segments (like a pie!) to represent different elements of the whole.

The origins of Jamaicans and the people of Trinidad and Tobago are shown in your *Caribbean School Atlas* by pie graphs (see **pages 30 and 49**). In each case, the circle represents the total population and the segments represent the continents their ancestors arrived from. What does the pie chart on **page 52** show?

Vertical bar graph

Information is shown by vertical bars. Each bar is proportional in length to the volume it represents. The scale is usually to the left of the bars. At the base of the graph there will be a key to what it is that is being compared.

> ⏰ Look at the climate graphs for the Caribbean region on atlas **page 20**. Each graph has twelve vertical bars. On the left axis is the key to what is represented by a bar (in millimetres of rain per month). At the base of the graph you will see that each bar represents a month. If we look at the graph for Limon, for example, we can see that the city receives on average over 500 millimetres of rainfall in October. How many millimetres of rain fall in Limon in February?
> ....

Horizontal bar graph

Information is shown by horizontal bars. The scale is usually at the base of the graph, below the bars. To the left or right of the graph there will be a key to what the bars represent.

12 Interpreting graphs

There is a horizontal **bar graph** on atlas **page 51**. It shows how the production of selected products in Trinidad changed over the ten years between 2004 and 2014. Some increased. Some decreased. You will see that for some products, there was a drop in output in 2014 compared with 2004. But six products increased in output. Can you name these six?

Look also at the age distribution pyramid for Jamaica on **page 30**. The pyramid comprises two horizontal bar graphs: the left one for males; the right one for females. Each bar shows the percentage for one gender that falls in a particular age group. You will see that the shortest bar is for men aged over 80 years. Only about 2 per cent of Jamaicans are men aged 80 and over. It is a bigger percentage for women. This kind of graph is called a **population pyramid** and is often used to compare female and male populations of a country.

Pictorial graph

Information is presented using a picture to represent a quantity. This is intended to make it easier for the reader to interpret the graph. There are no pictorial graphs in your *Caribbean School Atlas*.

If we convert the line and bar graph on atlas **page 52** into a pictorial graph, this is what it would look like. Each barrel represents a million tonnes of crude oil. Each gas cylinder represents 10 billion cubic metres of natural gas extracted. Which kind of graph is easiest for you to understand?

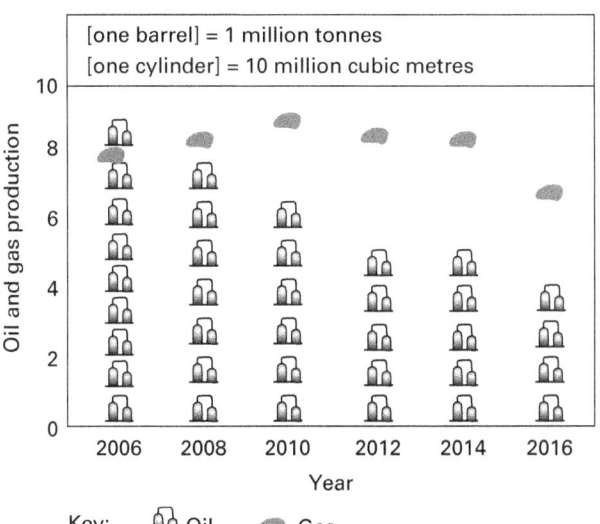

Oil and gas production, 2006–2016

Divided bar graph

In this kind of graph, the bar represents the whole, or 100 per cent. It is divided into sections. Let's consider ancestral origins. The origins of Jamaicans and the people of Trinidad and Tobago are shown in your *Caribbean School Atlas* by pie graphs (see **pages 30 and 49**).

We could show the same information by two divided bar graphs like those below. It is easier to compare the information for two countries with two divided bars than with two pie graphs. In what ways are the two countries similar and different in terms of the origins of their population?

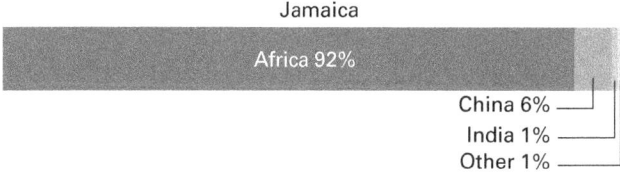

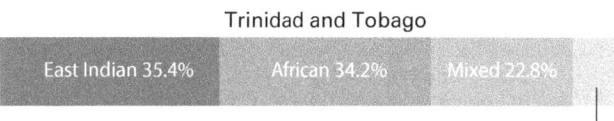

Origins of the populations of Jamaica (top) and Trinidad and Tobago (bottom)

Flow chart

A **flow chart** uses bars with an arrowhead and bends them on a map to show the direction of flow. The width of the bar represents the volume. There are no flow charts in your *Caribbean School Atlas*.

Look at the flow of enslaved Africans transported to the Caribbean and the Americas on atlas **page 15** (top map). The lines are all the same width, so you cannot see which routes were largest or smallest. The map opposite also provides information about the transportation of Africans. But included in this map is a flow chart. It shows just how many Africans were taken across the Atlantic by force. The number is shown by the width of the bars. Can you see how many Africans were brought to Jamaica over the centuries? How many were transported to Guyana?

PART 2 INTERPRET DATA, GRAPHS AND PHOTOGRAPHS

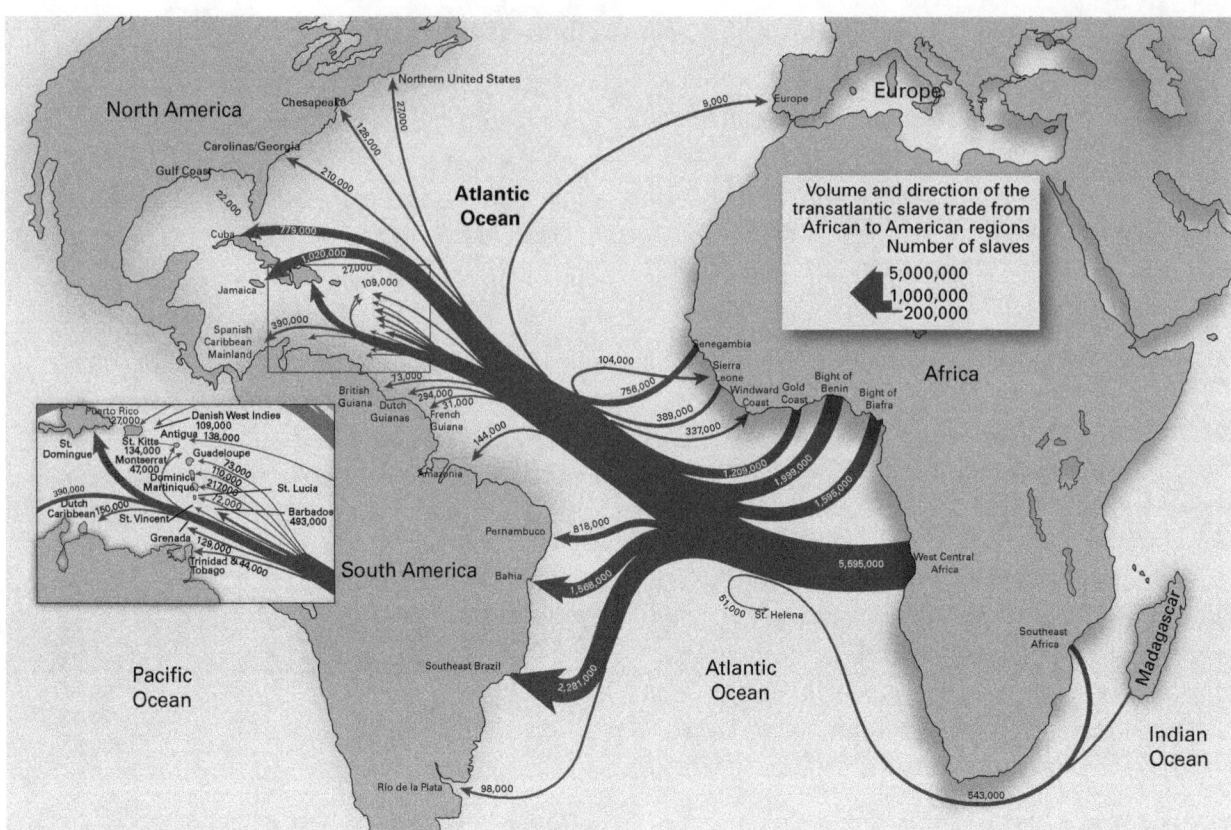

Volume and direction of the forced migration of Africans across the Atlantic Ocean between 1500 and 1860

Practice in interpreting graphs

For the following questions on four kinds of graph, first find the correct page in your *Caribbean School Atlas* and then fill in the correct answer.

Line graph

1. Which two months are hottest in Port-au-Prince? (graph, page 20)

   ....

2. Which of the places shown on page 78 with climate graphs has the driest climate?

   ....

3. What was the world's population in millions in 1825, 1925 and 2025? (graph, page 82)

   ....

Pie graph

4. What percentage of Jamaica's stopover tourists are from Canada? (pie graph, page 32)

   ....

5. What percentage of Jamaica's imports originated in Japan in 2016? (pie graph, page 32)

   ....

6. How much of Trinidad and Tobago's land is forested? (pie graph, page 51)

   ....

Vertical bar graph

7. Which Caribbean country's economy is most dependent on tourism? (lower graph, page 21)

   ....

   What percentage of its economy was from tourism in 2016?

   ....

8. Which Caribbean country had the smallest proportion of its employed people directly involved in tourism in 2016? (upper graph, page 21)

   ....

12 Interpreting graphs

9 Which of Jamaica's resort areas has the largest number of stopover tourists? (bar graph, page 32)

　..

10 Which place in Trinidad and Tobago has the highest rainfall in March? (bar graph, page 50)

　..

Horizontal bar graph

11 Which of Jamaica's agricultural crops produces about 140,000 tonnes? (graph, page 31)

　..

12 Name which of Trinidad's agricultural products showed an increase in production in 2014 compared with 2004. (page 51)

　..

Pyramid graph

13 Which of Trinidad and Tobago's age cohorts is largest for males and females? (pyramid graph, page 49)

　..

14 Which of Jamaica's age groups has the lowest proportion of males? (pyramid graph, page 30)

　..

QQ Quick quiz on interpreting graphs

Select the correct response for these quiz questions about data and diagrams in your atlas. Tick a, b, c or d.

1 This is not a type of statistical graph:
   a vertical bar graph ☐
   b pyramid graph ☐
   c photograph ☐
   d line graph ☐

2 The graph at the bottom of page 51 of your atlas is a:
   a line graph ☐
   b bar graph ☐
   c divided circle ☐
   d pictorial graph ☐

3 The divided circle for Trinidad and Tobago on page 51 of your atlas shows that:
   a most of the country is arable land ☐
   b forest covers nearly half of the country ☐
   c 5,000 square kilometres is used for permanent crops ☐
   d none of the land area is urban ☐

4 For all visitors to Trinidad and Tobago in 2016 (page 53):
   a 16 per cent arrived in cruise ships ☐
   b 84 per cent arrived in cruise ships ☐
   c 40 per cent of stopover tourists arrived from the USA ☐
   d Barbados and Grenada contributed 10 per cent of stopover tourists ☐

   ```
   Africa 92%
   China 6%
   India 1%
   Other 1%
   ```

5 The above type of graph is called a:
   a vertical bar graph ☐
   b horizontal bar graph ☐
   c pyramid graph ☐
   d divided bar graph ☐

PART 2 INTERPRET DATA, GRAPHS AND PHOTOGRAPHS

13 Photographs

NEW SKILL

Acquire skill in analysing photographs to interpret a scene and to recognise how photographs complement atlas maps and other data.

Types of photograph

Photographs record a scene at a moment in time. They were once complicated to take, expensive to process and taken by a skilled photographer. Today, photography is ubiquitous – everyone with a smartphone has a sophisticated camera, and photographs can be taken from the air and from space. Let's consider four basic kinds of photography.

Oblique landscape photography

This is a term we could use for traditional photographs taken from the ground by a photographer. There are lots of landscape photographs in your *Caribbean School Atlas*, such as the six photographs on **page 18**. Some landscape photographs include people and activities. But people in landscape photographs are not portraits. In landscape photographs, people have just been caught in their everyday activities at work, home or school.

Close-ups

Another form of photography is to make a portrait of a person or object. The photograph is carefully composed to show a detailed image of an individual person or object. Look at the photographs of Trinidad's national bird and national flower on **page 48**. This is close-up photography. The object is in the foreground. The middle ground and background are irrelevant to the shot.

These days, many people can take close-up portraits as selfies on their smartphones. Another example is the Crop-Over Carnival reveller in Barbados in the photograph on **page 46**. It is a close-up but it is intended to show a cultural tradition, not to be a portrait of the particular reveller!

Aerial photography

Photographs taken from some point above the Earth's surface from a helicopter, plane or drone are examples of aerial photography. These may be taken at an oblique or vertical angle. If vertical, the photograph is like a map, although the landscape is represented by actual objects and colours, not symbols.

Look at **page 27** in your *Caribbean School Atlas*. This photograph of Kingston in 2018 was commissioned especially for this atlas and was taken by a drone hovering over Kingston Harbour.

Satellite photography

Satellites take photographs of Earth from space. *Google Maps* uses satellite photography taken vertically above the landscape shown. Look at the satellite photographs in your *Caribbean School Atlas* on **pages 38 and 62**. One shows an image of a hurricane as it passes over the Caribbean. The other shows the world's biggest river (by volume of water) where it enters the Atlantic Ocean.

> Here are four photographs taken from your atlas. They are labelled A, B, C and D. Classify these according to type of photograph.
>
> A  B
>
> C  D
>
> 1 Oblique landscape photograph ....
>
> 2 Close-up shot ....
>
> 3 Aerial photograph ....
>
> 4 Satellite image ....

Foreground, middle ground and background

Many landscape-type photographs have three planes. The foreground of the composition is the visual plane that appears closest to the viewer. The background is the plane in a composition perceived furthest from the viewer. The middle ground is the visual plane located between both the foreground and background.

You will be able to identify these three planes in most landscape photographs in your atlas. These terms will be useful in undertaking your analysis of photographs. The three terms are demonstrated for the photograph below in the margins beside it.

Look at the landscape photograph on page 62 of your atlas, which is reproduced here in one colour. Part of Lake Titicaca is in the foreground. The Andes mountain range is in the background. In the middle ground are the low-lying, tree-covered hills between the lake and the mountain range.

Identifying foreground, middle ground and background of a composition

Interpreting photographs

You can learn a lot from careful interpretation of photographs. This is the skill of photograph interpretation. Let's begin by examining the photograph in the box on this page and see what we can learn from it.

We can examine:
- **Environment or context:** What was the weather like when the photograph was taken? What is the landscape in the background? What kind of climate? What time of day and time of year was the picture taken?
- **Objects in the picture:** What objects can you see? Do you recognise them? What is their purpose?
- **Human activity:** What are the people doing?

Based on these observations, we can draw conclusions from the scene.

This photo was taken in Taiwan. In your group, try to interpret this photograph by applying the above questions.

Now look at the answers below and see how your interpretation matches ours!
- **Environment or context:** The area is mountainous. The vegetation looks lush – so the rainfall is probably high. The hills have been contoured for growing a special crop. It looks misty and cool. Terracing the land is an old custom in tropical countries for growing special crops like rice, tea and coffee.
- **Objects in the picture:** We can see workers in the field. They are wearing straw conical hats to give protection from the Sun. These are typical of South and South East Asia. There is no equipment to help the workers do their job – typical of places with larger populations. There is a large building like a factory in the photograph. Perhaps the product is stored and processed there. Perhaps the workers sleep there.
- **Human activity:** The workers have baskets to collect something, but no machetes to cut or dig. They appear to use their hands to pick leaves from the bushes and put them into their baskets. We know that tea is grown on bushes and picked by hand. So we conclude that this may be tea grown on terraces and picked by hand. It will be carried to the factory for processing.

PART 2 INTERPRET DATA, GRAPHS AND PHOTOGRAPHS

Practice interpreting photographs

Interpret the photographs in your *Caribbean School Atlas* listed below and find the solution to each question. Try answering the questions before you check with the captions.

5 For the Notting Hill carnival picture (page 17) state in few words what is in the foreground, middle ground and background:

Foreground: ....

Middle ground: ....

Background: ....

6 Explain the activity happening in the Panama Canal photograph on page 10:

....

....

7 What objects appear white in the satellite image on page 13?

....

8 List six agricultural products of the Caribbean shown in the photographs on page 18:

i: ....   ii: ....   iii: ....

iv: ....   v: ....   vi: ....

More than 10 million tourists visit the Caribbean every year. Why do they come? Photographs can give us clues. Make a list of the reasons by finding attractions in the photographs on the following pages.

9 page 21: ....   14 page 39: ....

10 page 23: ....   15 page 46: ....

11 pages 25 and 42: ....   16 page 51, lower picture:

12 page 33: ....

13 page 37, both pictures: 17 page 53, both pictures:

....

Analyse the photographs of the hills of St Lucia (page 21), Montserrat (page 37) and Vanuatu (page 70) and answer these questions.

18 Are the hills similar in shape?

....

19 Why are they similar in shape?

....

20 How might the hills be tourist attractions?

....

21 When should tourists stay away?

....

13 Photographs

> There are four photographs in your *Caribbean School Atlas* showing important land and seascapes protected because of their natural beauty. Name the four protected sites.

22 Country ....

Site ....

23 Country ....

Site ....

24 Country ....

Site ....

25 Country ....

Site ....

QQ Quick quiz on interpreting photographs

Select the correct response for these quiz questions about photographs. Tick a, b, c or d.

1 A photograph taken from a hilltop of the scene several kilometres away is:
   a an oblique landscape photograph ☐
   b a close-up shot ☐
   c an aerial photograph ☐
   d a satellite image ☐

2 Which part of the photograph on the right from atlas **page 39** is the middle ground?
   a A ☐
   b B ☐
   c C ☐
   d D ☐

3 One of Vanuatu's islands is shown in the photograph on atlas **page 70**. Which of the following statements about the scene is not correct?
   a The cloud may be caused by steam arising from the volcano's crater ☐
   b The shape of the island is typical of one formed by volcanic eruption ☐
   c The blue of the sea is a clear indication of active eruption ☐
   d Volcanic slurry has been deposited on the vegetation showing eruption was recent ☐

4 In the satellite image of the Great Barrier Reef on **page 71**, the coral reef appears as:
   a the dark blue areas ☐
   b the pale green areas ☐
   c the light blue lines in the dark blue areas ☐
   d the white areas between pale green and dark blue ☐

5 The feature at the centre of the right-hand photograph on **page 60** shows:
   a an explosion ☐
   b a human-made scene ☐
   c a waterfall ☐
   d a dam ☐

14 GAME BOX: DATA, GRAPHS AND PHOTOGRAPHS

SKILLS PRACTICE

Try these three activities and have fun practising the skills you have acquired. The games cover: analysing photographs and interpreting data.

Carnival time!

Here are photographs of carnivals in Rio de Janeiro in Brazil, Port of Spain in Trinidad, Bridgetown in Barbados and London in England. One of these is not in your *Caribbean School Atlas*. Work in a pair and find which carnival is not shown by a photograph in your atlas!

Waving the right flags!

There are two pairs of countries in the world that have nearly identical flags. Hunt through the world's flags on **pages 73 to 75** to find them! Here is a clue: One pair of identical flags has a vertical red stripe and the other pair has a horizontal red stripe.

The two pairs of countries are:

a .... and ....

b .... and ....

Create a picture of your class by a statistical table

Collect information about every student in your class by the simple hands-up method! For example: Hands up how many girls were born on Sunday? Hands up how many boys were born on Sunday? How many don't know? Perhaps the data for 40 students would be: 5 girls; 2 boys; 31 don't know; and 2 absent from class!

Your teacher will help you select a few interesting questions. Write the data for the class on the chalkboard. Then use the data to make a table about the characteristics of your class of students.

15 Data, graphs and photographs test

SKILLS ASSESSMENT

This test checks data and graph skills you acquired in Chapters 12 to 14.

Use your *Caribbean School Atlas* to find the correct answer. Only one of the four possible answers given is correct. Tick either A, B, C or D.

1. These islands are an independent country:
   - A Turks and Caicos Islands
   - B Trinidad and Tobago
   - C St Vincent and the Grenadines
   - D United States Virgin Islands

2. The estimated population of Guyana in 2018 was:
   - A almost 750,000
   - B over 750,000
   - C almost 214,970
   - D over 214,970

3. Bauxite mining is a major industry of:
   - A Trinidad
   - B The Bahamas
   - C Belize
   - D Guyana

4. The city in Asia with the largest population is:
   - A Shanghai
   - B Tokyo
   - C Beijing
   - D Delhi

5. Use the Countries Facts & Figures table on **pages 73 to 75** to find which of the following counties is 103,000 square kilometres in area.
   - A Egypt
   - B Mexico
   - C Tonga
   - D Iceland

6. The diagram below shows the distances of planets from the Sun (see **page 76**). The names have been replaced with letters. Circle the planet that is Jupiter.

   A   B   C   D

7. The production of oil in Trinidad and Tobago in 2012 (**page 52**) was:
   - A 26 billion cubic metres
   - B 42 billion cubic metres
   - C 6 million tonnes
   - D 26 million tonnes

8. The percentage of Jamaicans who live in rural areas (**page 30**) is:
   - A 45 per cent
   - B 35 per cent
   - C 92 per cent
   - D 20 per cent

9. The largest cohort of the population of Trinidad and Tobago (**page 49**) is aged:
   - A 0–9 years
   - B 10–19 years
   - C 20–29 years
   - D 30–39 years

10. The photograph on **page 10** shows:
    - A a port in Panama
    - B cruise ships transporting tourists to the Caribbean
    - C lock gates of a canal to raise and lower ships
    - D a shipbuilding yard

11. What is common to the six photographs on **page 18**?
    - A All crops are grown on lowlands
    - B Only men are involved in harvesting
    - C All crops are harvested by hand
    - D All are food crops

12. What type of photograph is on **page 27**?
    - A An oblique landscape photograph
    - B A close-up shot
    - C An aerial photograph
    - D A satellite image

PART 3 INTERPRET THEMATIC MAPS

16 Maps of natural patterns

NEW SKILL

Acquire skills in interpreting thematic maps that show patterns of seismic activity, topography, seasons, rainfall, temperature, hurricanes and time zones, across continents and countries. Understand why the natural environment must be conserved. Be able to calculate the time in other countries of the world.

Plate, earthquake and volcano patterns

The surface of our planet Earth is made of many moving plates. These are shown on atlas **pages 12 and 81**. You will see that the Caribbean is on a small plate boxed in by other plates. As the plates crush together or move apart, they cause earthquakes and the eruption of volcanoes. These, in turn, may cause tsunamis.

Study these two pages of the atlas and complete the following sentences.

1. The Caribbean Plate is between the .... Plate to the north, the .... Plate to the east and south, and the .... Plate and .... Plate to the south-west. (page 12)

2. Jamaica was last affected by a major tsunami in the year .... (page 12)

3. To the east of the eastern Caribbean islands is a deep ocean trench named .... (page 12)

4. There was a major earthquake in .... in 2016. (page 81)

5. When molten .... is forced up through the pipe of a volcano, it erupts through the .... and spills over the edge. (page 81)

6. The continent which does not have a zone of earthquake risk is .... (page 81)

7. The African Plate is between the .... Plate to the north, the .... and .... plates to the east, and the .... and .... plates to the west. (page 81)

8. Most earthquakes in the Caribbean and the world occur where .... meet. (pages 12 and 81)

Fill in the captions on this cross-section. The original diagram is on atlas **page 81**.

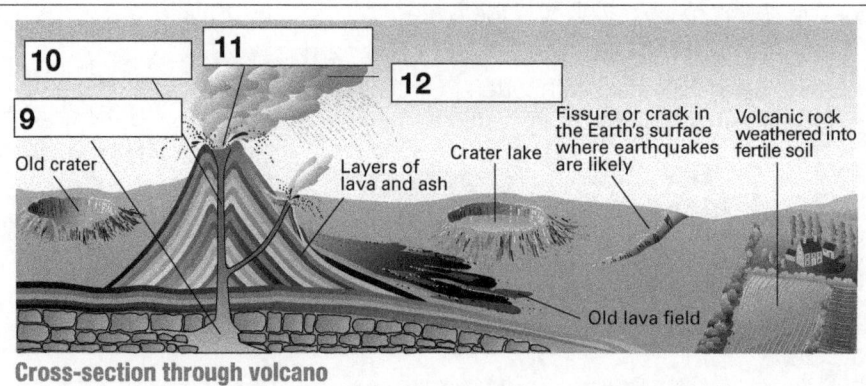

Cross-section through volcano

16 Maps of natural patterns

Topography

The world map across **pages 56 and 57** enables us to see at a glance the topography of land areas and sea. The major mountain ranges and the major trenches below the seas and oceans are shown by tints. There are fact files at the bottom of **page 57** on the world's largest, longest, deepest and highest features.

> Use these pages to answer the following questions.
>
> 13 Name the major mountain ranges of North America, Central America, South America and central Asia:
>
>   ....
>
> 14 In which ocean is the world's deepest trench?
>
>   ....
>
> 15 Which ocean borders eastern Africa, southern Asia and western Australia?
>
>   ....
>
> 16 Which is the largest island of Africa?
>
>   ....
>
> 17 How many mountain peaks are more than 5,000 metres high?
>
>   ....

The atlas also has a larger-scale map of the topography of every continent. Let's look at the map of Africa on **page 64**, for example. Its scale is 1:67,000,000, a larger scale than the world map at 1:100,000,000. The key to tints is also different. Some areas shown as green in Africa on the world map may be yellow on the continent map. There is much more detail on the larger-scale map.

> Use the Africa map on atlas **page 64** to complete these sentences on the continent's topography.
>
> 18 The .... Mountains in northern Africa are between .... and .... metres above sea level.
>
> The .... Highlands in eastern Africa are higher, with many parts higher than 4,000 metres.
>
> 19 Lake Tanganyika lies along the north–south split in the continent's surface called the .... Valley.
>
> 20 The southernmost point of Africa is called the ....

For every Caribbean country, the atlas provides a topographical map. Let's look at the map for Guyana on **page 54** and practise the skill of interpreting a country's topography.

> Here is a smaller version of the map of Guyana with some dotted lines to guide you. Your task is to make a simple sketch map of the country's topography following these six steps:
> - Tint the Pakaraima Mountains and the Kanuku Mountains brown.
> - Tint the swampy areas light blue (these are labelled mangroves in the key).
> - Draw in Guyana's main rivers in dark blue – Mazaruni, Essequibo, Demerara, Berbice and Corentyne.
> - Tint the other areas light green.
> - Label the two mountain areas and the five rivers.

PART 3 INTERPRET THEMATIC MAPS

Seasons

The top diagram on **page 77** shows how planet Earth revolves around the Sun. At the same time, it is rotating on its axis. The imaginary lines sticking out of the North and South poles show you that the axis on which the Earth rotates is tilted at an angle of 23.5° in relation to the Sun's orbital plane.

In a group of two, act out the scene in the Year & Seasons diagram. One student is the Sun and stands still in the middle of a circle radiating solar energy in all directions. The other student represents the Earth.

The Earth student moves (revolves) around the Sun in 365 days. At the same time, he or she rotates once every 24 hours!

Start when it is 21 March. When Earth has revolved a quarter way, it will be 21 June. Another quarter, it will be 23 September. What date is the northern winter/southern summer?

By play-acting the way that Earth rotates on its axis and at the same time revolves around the Sun you will better understand the Year & Seasons diagram.

Now complete the following sentences.

21 Earth's axis is titled at .... degrees in relation to the Sun and as a result we have four distinct .... every complete revolution.

22 Earth takes .... days to make one complete revolution around the Sun.

23 The sequence of seasons is: .... follows winter, summer follows ...., ... follows summer, and .... follows ....

24 In Australia, in the southern hemisphere, the middle of summer falls on 21 ....

Rainfall maps and graphs

Your *Caribbean School Atlas* gives you information about the climate of countries and regions, including the amount of rain that falls and when, the temperature and hurricanes that affect the Caribbean. We begin by looking at rainfall maps and graphs.

Look at the pattern of the world's rainfall on **page 79**. Say how many millimetres of rain falls in a year in:

25 Africa, at the Tropic of Cancer: ....

26 Indonesia: ....

27 Florida, USA: ....

Use the words in the key to the rainfall map on **page 79** to complete these sentences.

28 Places in Africa range from those where the average annual rainfall is under .... to those where the average is more than ....

29 There is no place along the Equator that has less than .... of rainfall a year.

Now turn to the maps of Jamaica's rainfall on **page 31**.

30 Which parish has the heaviest rainfall for both six-month periods? ....

31 Which two areas of Jamaica have the lowest annual rainfall? ....

32 Examine the four climate graphs and find which month has the highest rainfall in Cinchona Gardens and Port Antonio: ....

33 Which months are driest in Montego Bay? ....

34 How much rain falls on average in a year in Port Antonio? .... mm per year

35 What direction do Jamaica's prevailing winds come from? .... and ....

16 Maps of natural patterns

Look at Trinidad and Tobago's rainfall map and rainfall graphs on page 50.

36 Which direction do Trinidad's winds come from? ....

37 Name the three hills in Trinidad and Tobago that receive over 2,500 millimetres of rainfall. (Compare the map on page 50 with those on page 48.) ....

38 Which month at Piarco has the greatest number of rain days? ....

39 Which month at Crown Point in Tobago has the lowest number of rain days? ....

Temperature maps and graphs

The world's temperature patterns are mapped on pages 78 and 79.

The two temperature maps on page 79 tell you how warm or cold it is on average in different regions in January and July.

The map on page 78 defines nine types of climate and shows which places have each type of climate. Make use of these two pages to answer the following questions.

Which city, of those marked on the map of climate types (page 78), has each of the following types of climate?

40 Humid tropical climate: ....

41 Continental climate: ....

42 Polar climate: ....

Using one of the nine broad climate types, describe the climate of:

43 The Caribbean islands: ....

44 The British Isles: ....

45 The south-eastern USA: ....

46 The Sahara desert: ....

Look at the temperature graphs on page 78 and complete the following sentences.

47 The average January temperature of Singapore is .... and of Anchorage is ....

48 .... is the month when average temperatures in Perth are highest.

49 The curve of the temperature graph for Buenos Aires is typical of places .... of the Equator.

50 The difference between summer and winter temperatures is .... degrees at Edmonton.

  Complete the table about the nine types of climate. The first example has been completed for you.

City	Average annual rainfall	Climate type	Description
Singapore	2,413 mm	Humid tropical	Hot with rain all year
Lima			
Nassau			
Edmonton			
Buenos Aires			
Quebec			
	372 mm	Subarctic	Very cold winter
Eismitte			
Addis Ababa			

PART 3 INTERPRET THEMATIC MAPS

Climate and natural vegetation

When rainfall patterns and temperature patterns are combined, we can summarise the result as a climate type. There are many ways of defining climate types. Your *Caribbean School Atlas* identifies nine types of climate. These are named in the key and specified in the map on **page 78**. The fifteen graphs below the map have been selected to illustrate the temperature and rainfall patterns for each climate type.

> Closely related to climate types is the pattern of natural vegetation on **page 80** of your *Caribbean School Atlas*. Eleven types of natural vegetation are shown on the map. Use the climate and natural vegetation maps (**pages 78 and 80**) together and write down the vegetation type to match each climate type.
>
> 51 Climate type: Polar Vegetation type:
>
>   Vegetation type: ....
>
> 52 Climate type: Humid tropical
>
>   Vegetation type: ....
>
> 53 Climate type: Subarctic
>
>   Vegetation type: ....
>
> 54 Climate type: Hot desert
>
>   Vegetation type: ....
>
> 55 Climate type: Steppe
>
>   Vegetation type: ....

Hurricanes

> The maps and tables on atlas **page 13** show how hurricanes affect the Caribbean. Use these to answer the following questions.
>
> 56 Which of these countries is most at risk of being hit by a hurricane in any one year: Trinidad and Tobago, Haiti or Belize?
>
>   ....
>
> 57 Which countries did the eye of hurricane Jeanne pass over in 2004? ....
>
>   ....

58 In which direction did the path of hurricane Dennis head through the Caribbean in 2005? From .... to ....

59 In which direction was the path of hurricane Sandy through the Caribbean in 2012? From .... to ....

60 Based on the table showing nine major hurricanes, which three months of the year are most at risk? ....

    ....

61 Which hurricane shown on the map did not begin in the Atlantic Ocean?

    ....

62 What category would a hurricane be if its winds are 200 km/hour? ....

63 How strong are winds in a Category 4 hurricane? From .... to ....

64 What category was hurricane Irma, shown in the satellite image (bottom right), when it passed over Barbuda? ....

    ....

Use the cross-section through a hurricane at the bottom of **page 13** to complete these sentences.

65 A hurricane may cover an area from 200 to .... kilometres.

66 The system may be .... kilometres high.

67 Air moves upwards at the ...., cooling as it ...., and creating dense ....

68 The .... at the centre of the hurricane is ....

16 Maps of natural patterns

Environmental concerns

⏰ Some key environmental concerns of the world are highlighted on atlas **page 80**. These are pollution, deforestation and desertification. Which of these terms best fits the major environmental concern of each of the following places? You will have to compare the map on **page 80** with the countries of the world map on **pages 58 and 59**.

69 Western Australia: ....

70 Brazil: ....

71 The Mediterranean Sea: ....

72 Western part of USA: ....

73 Botswana: ....

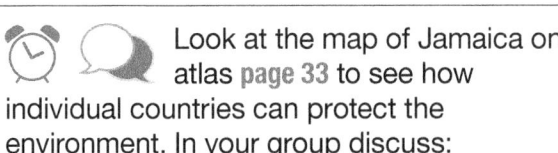 Look at the map of Jamaica on atlas **page 33** to see how individual countries can protect the environment. In your group discuss:
- what the Government of Jamaica did in 2017 to protect the Cockpit Country
- what UNESCO is doing to encourage countries to conserve their environments
- what biodiversity hotspots are
- what is the link between the environment and the tourist industry.

Time zones

Planet Earth continually rotates. It completes one rotation every 24 hours. This is the basis of our measurement of time. Some places see dawn 24 hours later than other places!

Look at the diagrams illustrating day and night on atlas **page 77**. You can see the Earth's axis, tilted always at 23.5° in respect to the Sun. Due to the tilted axis, even places on the same line of longitude do not have dawn at the same time.

For everyone to be able to think of midnight where they live as 00:00 hours, and midday as 12:00 hours, the concept of **time zones** was developed in the middle of the nineteenth century and adopted universally about 100 years ago. The Greenwich Meridian is the base line and gives Greenwich Mean Time, or GMT. The zone extends either side of 0°.

All other longitudinal zones are defined as before or after GMT. If it is before GMT, it is shown with a +. Sydney, Australia, has midnight ten hours before London so it is +10. If it is after GMT, it is shown with a –. Midnight in Miami is five hours after London, so it is –5.

Page 7 of your *Caribbean School Atlas* is a map of the world's time zones. Read the explanation under the map.

⏰ Use the map on atlas **page 7** to make your own time zone map for CARICOM countries. Imagine it is noon in Suriname and write in the time for each of the other zones in the box provided.

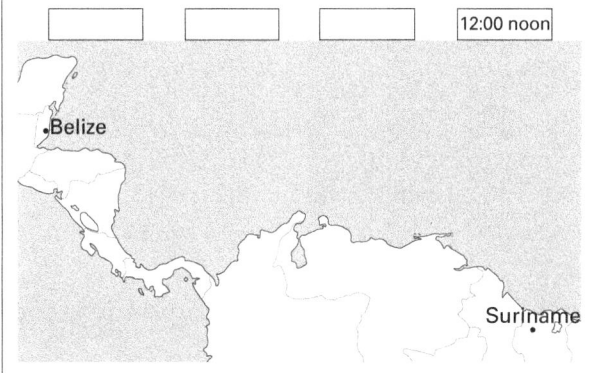

⏰ Now complete the following sentences.

74 The world is divided into .... time zones.

75 Near to the South Pole, each time zone is .... degrees of longitude wide.

76 Zones do not always follow lines of .... exactly but are adjusted to take into account the special needs of each country involved.

77 The whole of the country .... has the same time (GMT +8) from east to west.

78 The hour of the day in Jamaica is always one hour .... (ahead or behind) the time in Trinidad and Tobago.

79 When it is 8 a.m. in Guyana, it is .... in London.

80 The countries of CARICOM are in a total of .... different time zones.

81 Africa is divided into .... time zones.

PART 3 INTERPRET THEMATIC MAPS

82 When it is midnight in Abidjan, it is .... in Tokyo.

83 When it is 7 a.m. in Miami, it is .... in Los Angeles.

Calculate the time in each of the following cities when the time is noon in Mexico City.

84 Dallas: ....

85 Rio de Janeiro: ....

86 Addis Ababa: ....

87 Delhi: ....

Calculate the time in Jamaica when it is:

88 3:30 p.m. in London, England: ....

89 Noon in Bangkok, Thailand: ....

90 4 p.m. in Sydney, Australia: ....

Some time zones are not a full hour different from GMT. Some countries prefer to use half- or quarter-hour differences. Find examples of these on the time zones map.

91 The time in Adelaide in central Australia is .... hours ahead of the time in Perth, western Australia.

92 When it is noon across the whole of India, it is .... in China.

93 Nepal is .... hours and .... minutes ahead of GMT.

QQ Quick quiz on the natural patterns

Select the correct response for these quiz questions about natural patterns. Tick a, b, c or d.

1 Which of the following statements is correct?
   a The Caribbean does not have volcanic eruptions
   b Earthquakes always occur in the summer months
   c The Earth's crust is fixed and does not move
   d The Caribbean is on a small plate boxed in by other plates

2 Average rainfall and temperature in Barbados in October (**page 47**) are respectively:
   a 150 mm and 27°C
   b 175 mm and 27°C
   c 17 mm and 157°C
   d 17 mm and 150°C

3 Which one of these was characteristic of hurricane Irma? (**page 13**)
   a It devastated Dominica
   b It was a category 4 storm
   c It originated in the southern Caribbean
   d Its winds were up to 295 km/hour

4 Which of the following statements related to climate is correct? (see **pages 78 and 79**)
   a In the northern and southern hemispheres summer is in July
   b South America is the hottest continent in July
   c Most of Indonesia has more than 3,000 millimetres of rainfall a year
   d Most of Africa has a continental climate

5 Which of these places is not a protected natural environment in Jamaica? (see **page 33**)
   a Parish of St Mary
   b Blue Mountains
   c Portland Ridge and Bight
   d The Cockpit Country

17 Maps of human-made patterns

 NEW SKILL

Acquire skills in interpreting thematic maps that show historical movements, population distribution and boundaries. Understand why these human-made patterns are significant in our lives.

Historical movements of people

Look at the spread of maps on atlas **pages 14 to 15**. These maps show you where people of the Caribbean originated and where they have migrated to. Use the four maps to answer the following questions.

1. Use the top map on **page 14** to name four Amerindian peoples who inhabited the Caribbean region in the era of European exploration and early annexation.

   ....
   ....

2. Which present-day countries were not conquered by the Spanish in the sixteenth century? Identify two of Jamaica, Trinidad, Barbados, the Bahamas, Cuba, Haiti, Belize or Puerto Rico from the lower map on **page 14**. .... and ....

3. How many people were transported across the Atlantic from Africa to the Caribbean before the prohibition of slave trading and slavery?

   ....

4. How many rebellions of enslaved Africans are noted on the top map on **page 15**?

   ....

5. In how many countries of the Caribbean has the United States intervened in the most recent era (according to the lower map on **page 15**)? ....

6. Using the lower map on **page 15**, find which of the following regions has not been a major destination for Caribbean migration: North America, Central America, northern part of South America, west Africa, European countries.

   ....

Work in groups of four to make up a story of twelve sentences about the people of the Caribbean, based only on facts shown in the four maps. Share the stories you create with your class.

Population distribution

Look at atlas **page 82**. The map shows where the world's population lives. One graph shows how the world population is growing. The bar graph compares the continents in terms of world population. The table lists the world's eight largest cities. The photo is of the largest city of all with a population of nearly 40 million people.

Use the sources of information on atlas **page 82** to answer the following questions.

7. What is the population of the world? About

   ....

8. By how many times has the world's population grown in the 200 years since 1825?

   ....

9. Which one of these places does not have a high concentration of population? India, western Australia, eastern China, eastern USA.

   ....

10. Which one of these places has a very low concentration of population? Central America, central Europe, northern Asia, the Indian subcontinent.

    ....

PART 3 INTERPRET THEMATIC MAPS

11 Which continent has most cities of 20 million or more people?

....

12 Which continent does not have a single city of 10 million people?

....

13 Which continent has the largest population?

....

14 How many continents have more people than North America?

....

⏰ The next questions are about Jamaica's population. Examine the population information on atlas **page 30** and complete these sentences.

15 There are .... cities and towns in Jamaica with more than 100,000 inhabitants.

16 The pie graph shows that .... (less than a half, one half, more than a half) of Jamaicans live in rural areas.

17 The part of Jamaica where the *population density* is lowest is .... (southern St Mary, southern Clarendon, southern Westmoreland).

18 The percentage of Jamaicans who are between 10 and 29 years of age is approximately .... per cent (10, 18, 36, 72).

⏰ Now turn to the population information for Trinidad and Tobago on atlas **page 49**.

19 How many people live, on average, in every square kilometre in the corridor that stretches from Port of Spain to Arima?

....

20 Comparing the map of population density of Trinidad on **page 49** with the map of key areas of the island on **page 50**, which two of these areas have a population density of less than 100 persons per square kilometre? .... and ....

21 How many people, per square kilometre, live in the historic county of St David?

....

22 Count how many cities and towns are there in Trinidad with over 20,000 inhabitants. ....

23 What happened to the growth of the country's population in 1990? ....

24 What are the percentages of Trinidadians and Tobagonians whose ancestors are African or Indian? .... per cent and .... per cent

Administrative boundaries

Every country is divided into several parts for administration at the local level. A part of a country is marked by an internal boundary. The boundaries of such divisions are shown for each of the Caribbean countries, as they are important to the people of a country.

Countries use various names for divisions. For example, the USA consists of 50 states. Canada is divided into provinces. France is divided into *départements*. English-speaking countries in the Caribbean are divided into parishes or provinces or counties or districts or regions.

17 Maps of human-made patterns 63

Here is an outline map of Trinidad's local government boundaries. The boundaries are the same as those of the tinted map on atlas **page 49** showing the island's regions and boroughs. Three areas are numbered on the outline map. Complete the names of these administrative divisions in the key.

Key

25 City of ....

26 Borough of ....

27 Region of ....

Examine maps showing the internal boundaries of countries in the Caribbean section of your atlas and complete the following sentences.

28 Trinidad is now divided into .... cities, ... regions and .... boroughs.

29 Historically, Trinidad was divided into .... counties.

30 The island of .... is divided into three parishes: St Peter, St George's and St Anthony.

31 The districts of .... and .... were named when the French occupied the country (clues: *vieux* in French means 'old' and *gros* means 'big').

32 Ten islands have an administrative division named St George. These are:

....

....

....

33 You can stand at the peak of .... where the island's five parishes join.

34 In .... there is a district with the same name as the country itself.

Internal boundaries are usually shown on the landscape maps of Caribbean countries. This means that you can, for example, look at the landscape map and find out in which parish a town is located.

Look at the two maps of Barbados on **page 46** and find answers to these questions.

35 In which parish is Bridgetown located?

....

36 In which parish is Mile and a Quarter found?

....

37 Which is the most important town in St James parish?

....

38 Which parish has boundaries with St Thomas, St Joseph, St John, St Philip, Christchurch and St Michael?

....

You should know all the divisions of your own country! Find the outline map of your country online, print a copy, and write in the name of all your country's internal divisions.

PART 3 INTERPRET THEMATIC MAPS

Geographical regions

As well as having internal administrative boundaries, a country or island may be divided into geographical regions that reflect the landscape or human activities.

Look at the map of places in Trinidad on **page 50**. This shows the island divided into six broad regions: North, North Western, Central, South, East Coast and the East–West Corridor between Port of Spain and Sangre Grande. This is how Trinidadians refer to where they live and work, although these are not the official administrative areas. These are geographical regions.

Study the maps of Trinidad and select the correct response for the following questions.

39 Chaguanas is in the geographical region of Trinidad known as

....

40 The Nariva Swamp is in which geographical region – East Coast, East–West Corridor, North Western or Central?

....

41 Trinidad's highest mountain, El Cerro del Aripo, is in North Western, Central, South or North? ....

QQ Quick quiz on interpreting human-made patterns

Select the correct response for these quiz questions about interpreting human-made patterns. Tick a, b, c or d.

1 Which of the following statements is correct? (page 14)
   a When Columbus arrived in the Caribbean, there were only 2,000 Amerindian inhabitants ☐
   b The Amerindian inhabitants of the Caribbean islands migrated north from South America ☐
   c The Spanish captured the island of Hispaniola over 1,000 years ago ☐
   d The Mayan Civilisation was centred on Florida in North America ☐

2 This Caribbean country gains more people through immigration than it loses through emigration each year. (page 17)
   a Cayman Islands ☐
   b Jamaica ☐
   c Barbados ☐
   d Cuba ☐

3 The ridge of the Maya Mountains of Belize (page 23) forms a boundary between the following districts:
   a Belize and Guatemala ☐
   b Stann Creek and Toledo ☐
   c San Ignacio and Belmopan ☐
   d Cayo and Toledo ☐

4 The west coast of southern Africa (page 82) is characterised in global terms as a region of:
   a dense population ☐
   b uninhabited land ☐
   c low population density ☐
   d very large cities ☐

5 St Kitts and Nevis (page 39) is divided into:
   a 14 districts ☐
   b 9 districts ☐
   c 5 districts ☐
   d 2 districts ☐

18 Maps of economic activities

NEW SKILL
Utilising thematic maps in your atlas, interpret patterns of economic activities such as farming, fishing, manufacturing and tourism.

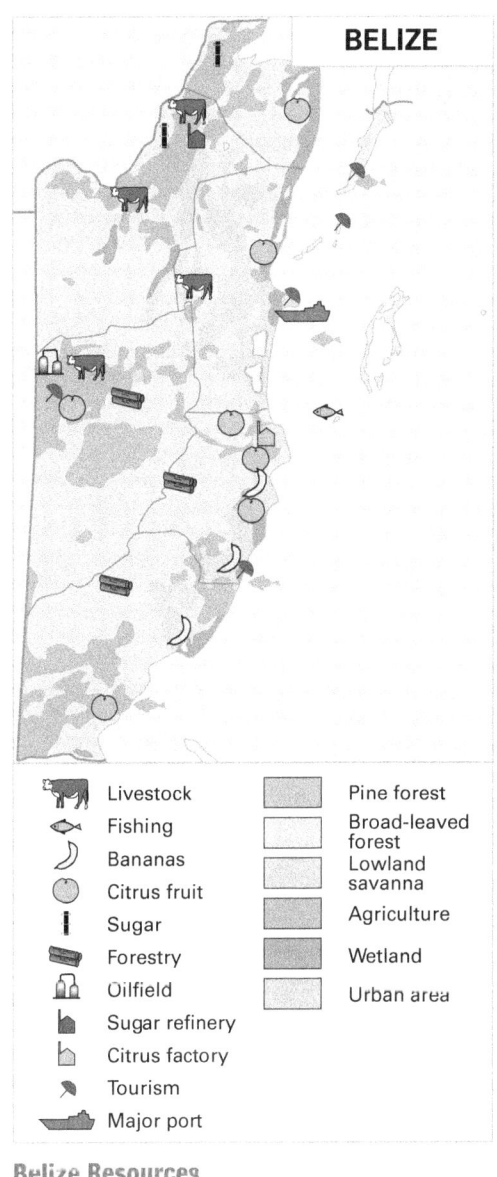

Belize Resources

For many of the larger CARICOM countries, your *Caribbean School Atlas* provides information on economic activities, sometimes in a single thematic map entitled Resources (see for example Belize, **page 23**), or in several maps (such as for Jamaica, **pages 31 and 32**).

These maps show patterns such as:
- natural resources; for example minerals and their extraction
- types of agricultural activities, important crops grown and livestock reared
- factories for processing minerals and agricultural products
- industrial areas with many factories and offices
- tourism areas and activities for tourists.

These economic activities provide employment for the people of a country. Colours and symbols are used to show where in a country such resources are concentrated. We can learn a lot about a country by studying maps of resources and economic activities.

Let's analyse the Resources map of Belize on atlas **page 23**.

1. Which district has a large pine forest?
   ....

2. About how much of the country is used for agriculture? (20 per cent, 40 per cent, 60 per cent, 80 per cent)
   ....

3. Which part of the country is urban?
   ....

4. Which two activities are important in Ambergris Cay in the north-west of the country?
   .... and ....

5. Belize's major port is in the district of
   ....

PART 3 INTERPRET THEMATIC MAPS

Tourism

What do tourists do when they visit a Caribbean country? Let's take Trinidad and Tobago as an example. Look at the tourism map on atlas page 53 and replace the symbols in the following passage with words from the map and key.

Tourist attractions of Trinidad and Tobago

Tourists enjoy the 6 ...., 7 .... and 8 .... around the coastline. And they go inland to explore the 9 ...., the 10 .... and 11 .... Some tourists are keen to learn about the country's history and culture and visit a 12 .... Others participate in the annual carnival in 13 .... Other attractions for active visitors are walking in the 14 .... or the 15 .... And what better way to exercise and relax at the same time but at a 16 ....! Tourists arrive and leave at an 17 .... or at a 18 .... where local crafts can be purchased on departure.

Most hotels built to cater for tourists to Caribbean countries are built (1) close to a beautiful beach by the sea, and (2) where the average rainfall is low. This is because most tourists come to the Caribbean in search of sun, sand and sea.

Look at the tourism and rainfall maps for Jamaica (pages 31 and 32) and Barbados (page 47) and find out whether or not the main tourist areas are near to the sea and located in areas where rainfall is low. Then complete the following sentences.

19 The main concentration of Jamaica's major hotel areas is along the island's .... coast.

20 The rainfall between Montego Bay and Oracabessa on Jamaica's north coast is between .... and .... millimetres per year.

21 The main tourism strip in Barbados is along the .... coast, where rainfall is between .... and .... millimetres per year.

Now make your own map of tourism areas in Jamaica using the outline map on the right.

Shade the coastal areas to show where tourist hotels are concentrated. The map on atlas page 32 will provide the information you need.

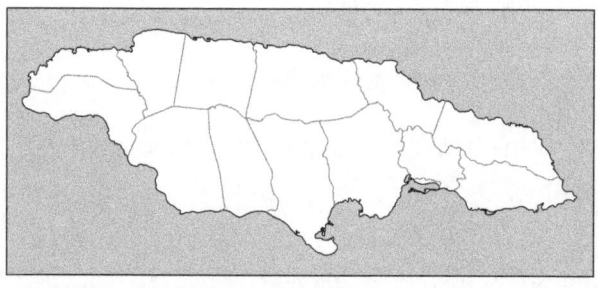

Jamaica's main tourism areas

Agriculture, mining and other economic activities

To get an idea of all the economic activities of Caribbean countries, we will look at ten maps and answer one question on each.

22 Jamaica Agriculture, page 31: What kind of land is used for growing sugar cane? (Compare with the topographical map on pages 26 to 27.)

....

18 Maps of economic activities

23 Jamaica Resources, page 32: Which three modes of transport take bauxite and alumina to other countries?

....

....

24 St Lucia Resources, page 42: Which parts of the country are covered with forest? (Compare with other maps of St Lucia on page 42.)

....

....

25 St Vincent Resources, page 43: Where in the island are bananas an important crop?

....

26 Guadeloupe Resources and Martinique Resources, page 40: How many rum distilleries are indicated for the two islands?

....

27 Grenada Resources, page 44: List five crops cultivated in Grenada:

....

....

28 Dominica Resources, page 41: Which three parishes are important for growing both coconuts and bananas?

....

....

29 Trinidad Resources, page 52: In which part of the island are land-based oilfields found?

....

30 Guyana Resources, pages 54 and 55: Which region has deposits of manganese?

....

Finally, let's look at the maps of Farming & Fishing across the world (atlas page 83) and see how the Caribbean region fits with world patterns. If you look at the top map, you will find that the Caribbean archipelago is tinted light green. This represents a region of commercial farming. And most of the Caribbean is not tinted deep blue – so it is not one of the world's principal fishing areas.

Other parts of the world have quite different agricultural systems. In small groups, discuss what you understand by the three kinds of land use mapped on page 83. Find in which parts of the world each one of the three is prominent:
- traditional hunting, fishing and gathering
- large-scale livestock ranching
- subsistence farming.

USING THE RIGHT MAPS FOR THE JOB

The Ministry of Education has funds to build one new school. The ministry's planning department is aware of changes in the distribution of the country's population. People are moving from rural farming communities to towns – where factories are located and where jobs are available.

a Select two thematic maps that government officers could examine to help in identifying the best location for a new school.

....

....

....

PART 3 INTERPRET THEMATIC MAPS

b What information could be obtained from the two maps you selected that could be useful in deciding on the best location for the new school to be built?

....

....

....

c What other information would the government need to make a decision on the best use of limited school construction funds?

....

....

....

QQ Quick quiz on maps of economic activities

Select the correct response for these quiz questions about maps of economic activities. Tick a, b, c or d.

1 Which of the following is not an example of an economic activity?
  a Natural resources such as forests, minerals and their extraction
  b Types of agricultural activities, important crops grown and livestock reared
  c Factories for processing minerals and agricultural products
  d Rainfall distribution across a country or region

2 The following is a major crop of Belize (page 23):
  a Citrus
  b Tobacco
  c Coconut
  d Nutmeg

3 Cocoa is grown in St Vincent (page 43):
  a in the highlands
  b along the north coast
  c in the parish of St George
  d in low-lying coastal areas

4 The most important area for tourists in Jamaica (page 32) is:
  a Montego Bay
  b Ocho Rios
  c Negril
  d The south coast

5 The location of Guyana's timber production (tinted brown on page 55) is unrelated to:
  a high rainfall enabling forest growth
  b large rivers enabling transportation
  c dense population enabling demand for produce
  d timber processing within main producing area

19 GAME BOX: INTERPRETING THEMATIC MAPS

 SKILLS PRACTICE

Try these six activities and have fun practising the skills you have acquired in Part 3 of your *Skills Workbook*. The games cover: tracking a hurricane that is a threat to the Caribbean, making your own population and resources maps, and finding places that have benefited through migration from the Caribbean migrants. You will also work out the time in cities across the world.

Hurricane alert

Most Caribbean countries are at risk of a hurricane hit each year during the hurricane season. This exercise is a real-time, real-life game learning the skill of recording the track of a hurricane day by day and trying to predict which countries will be affected by it.

You will have to do this during the hurricane season. The hurricane season for the Caribbean is the six months from June to November. You will have to start this exercise when you hear that a tropical storm presents a danger to the Caribbean. Find out the name that the storm has been given. Begin to record its progress. This exercise may take two weeks or more to complete, with a recording made in your log each day.

This is how a tropical disturbance becomes a hurricane:

Tropical disturbance
An area of thunderstorms moving forward in the tropics above an ocean or sea

↓

Tropical depression
The area of air moving in a circle increases in speed up to 61 km/hour (38 mph)

↓

Tropical storm
The speed of the circular air movement increases to between 62 and 117 km/hour (39 and 73 mph)

↓

Tropical hurricane
Circular movement of air now exceeds 118 km/hour (74 mph) and becomes very destructive

Track a hurricane as it moves!

To track the hurricane you have selected, work through the following steps.
- Find the hurricane-tracking chart on pages 102–103 of this workbook.
- Look at the hurricane daily observations log on page 101 and understand what information should be entered in each row.
- Write the name of the tropical storm in the space provided on the log and on the chart.
- Record information about the storm's position in the log. You will find information every day from media such as web, radio, newspaper, television and weather channels.
- Enter information for the first day you begin to track the hurricane as No.1 observation in the log.
- Record its position the next day as No.2 observation. Continue recording the coordinates of the hurricane until it disperses.
- Plot the daily positions of the hurricane's centre on the hurricane-tracking chart at the point where the latitude and longitude coordinates meet.
- Join each point plotted by a line. This is the track of the hurricane's eye (or centre).
- Try to assess which Caribbean countries will be affected (and how severely) as the hurricane moves forward day by day.

You can download copies of the hurricane tracking chart from the web page.

CARIBBEAN SCHOOL ATLAS
SKILLS WORKBOOK

Make your own population map

Let's make a population density map for Dominica. Use the outline map of the island below and follow the instructions.

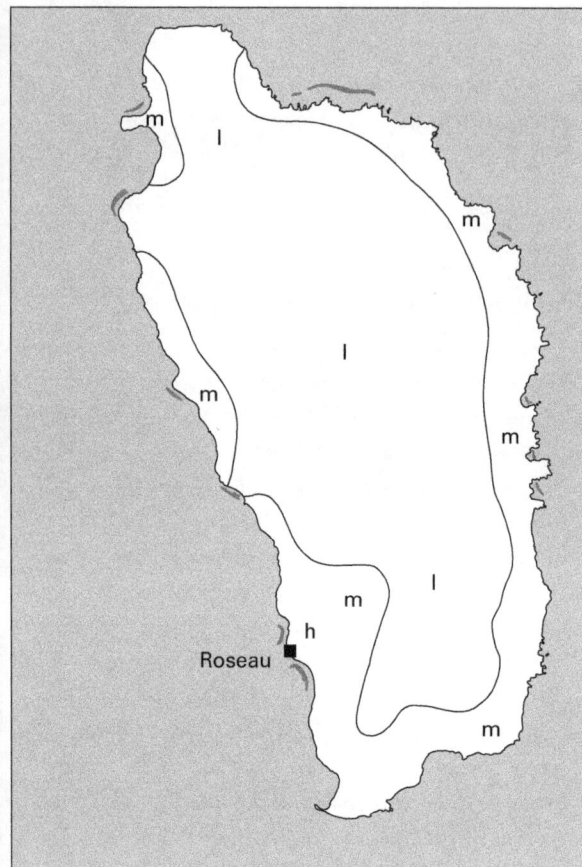

Dominica: population density

- Look at the areas marked on the map. The letters h, m and l correspond with letters in the key.
- Use the same tints as in the key of the Trinidad population density map on atlas **page 49**. Use yellow for low density, pale brown for medium density and brown for high density. Put the correct colours in the three boxes of the key.
- You can see there is only one high-density area, around Roseau, the capital. Shade it brown.
- Nearly all the other towns are around the coastline. Shade these medium-density areas in pale brown.
- All the other areas, the hills, have a low density. Shade these yellow.

Congratulations – you have made your first population density map! Is it as neat as the maps in your *Caribbean School Atlas*?

Thematic maps word search

Find the word hidden in the puzzle that fits each statement below. Some letters you will use twice. Shade in each word. You will create a shape when you have finished shading all seven words. Your clues are:

- The abbreviated form of the word SAINT used in many of the Caribbean country maps (**pages 23 to 55**).
- The name of a saint remembered in Dominica's south-eastern parish (**page 41**).
- The name of the parish in Barbados where the rainfall is highest (**pages 46 and 47**).
- The creature that gave its name to one of the gasfields east of Galeota Point in Trinidad (**page 52**).
- The capital of Jamaica (**pages 26 to 27**).
- A mineral found in the north-east of Guyana (**page 55**).
- Another word for wetland found along the east and west coasts of Trinidad and tinted purple (**page 51**).

H	C	G	F	H	W	I	D	V	S	G	R	S	L
D	P	D	O	L	P	H	I	N	R	H	T	X	G
Q	A	G	A	P	Y	F	R	N	X	K	R	D	A
W	T	H	D	V	P	N	B	N	E	Z	H	G	S
R	R	V	G	X	Z	Z	I	N	B	D	C	T	D
Y	I	F	H	E	S	T	T	H	O	M	A	S	F
U	C	X	C	H	T	T	E	K	S	D	F	D	G
S	K	I	N	G	S	T	O	N	J	F	D	L	G
G	S	S	N	L	W	H	S	Q	F	H	G	K	H
B	F	P	N	L	A	A	H	G	G	T	K	J	G
F	G	N	N	L	M	X	I	N	J	D	R	B	K
V	J	X	N	L	P	B	A	U	X	I	T	E	L
A	C	R	E	A	S	J	D	B	C	D	C	M	U

When you have shaded in all seven words, look at the Caribbean flags on **page 19** and find answers to these questions:

Which country's flag uses a shape or emblem like the one you found in the puzzle as part of its flag?

....

What do you think this emblem stands for?

....

Draw a resources map

Make your own resources map for the imaginary island of St Sebastian. An outline map of the island is below. Add a key using colours and symbols. Then tint the map and add the symbols in places indicated by the arrows. Use the same colours and symbols as are used in your *Caribbean School Atlas*.

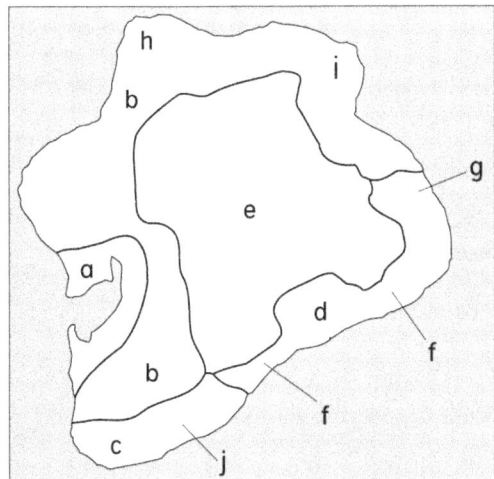

Find the Caribbean diaspora

Diaspora means the places settled outside the home region. This exercise is to find seven large cities in the USA and Canada (see atlas page 61) to which Caribbean people have emigrated over the past century. Fill in the missing letters horizontally to make your list of seven cities.

	I	A	I			
	E		O			
		I	A	O		
			A	A		
O		O		O		
	E		O	E	A	
	O		A	E		E

What time is it there?

Draw hands of the clock in the clock face labelled 'My country', to show the current time where you are. The long hand will show the minute, the short hand will show the hour.

Then use the map of time zones on atlas page 7 to draw the current time in Miami, Addis Ababa and Beijing.

For these cities, the minute hand will stay the same, and the hour hand will change. Under each clock, insert a.m. (before noon) or p.m. (after noon).

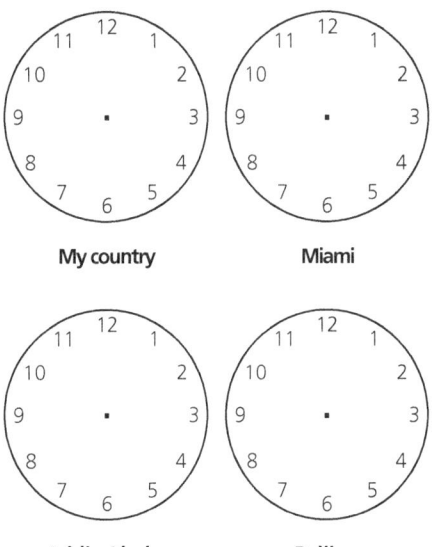

My country   Miami

Addis Ababa   Beijing

PART 3 INTERPRET THEMATIC MAPS

20 Test on thematic maps

SKILLS ASSESSMENT

This test checks skills you acquired in Chapters 16 to 19 related to the interpretation of thematic maps.

Use your *Caribbean School Atlas* to find the correct answers. Only one of the four possible answers given is correct. Tick A, B, C or D.

Answers to questions 1 to 4 can be found by using the topographical and thematic maps of St Lucia on atlas **page 42**.

1. The number of districts in St Lucia is:
   - A 9
   - B 10
   - C 11
   - D 12

2. The town of Marquis (B2) is in the parish of:
   - A Dauphin
   - B Gros Islet
   - C Dennery
   - D Castries

3. Most of the land over 200 metres high is used for:
   - A coconuts
   - B forestry
   - C bananas
   - D livestock farming

4. The tourist industry is located along the coasts of the parishes:
   - A Vieux Fort, Micoud
   - B Anse la Raye, Castries
   - C Castries, Micoud, Dauphin
   - D Castries, Gros Islet, Soufrière

Answers to questions 5 to 9 can be found on the maps of Jamaica (**pages 26 to 33**).

5. The parish of Hanover is in the county of:
   - A Surrey
   - B Middlesex
   - C Cornwall
   - D Westmoreland

6. The average rainfall at Hayes in Clarendon (F4) for the six months from November to April is:
   - A 2,000–3,000 millimetres
   - B 1,000–2,000 millimetres
   - C 500–1,000 millimetres
   - D under 500 millimetres

7. The average rainfall in Kingston in May is:
   - A 0 millimetres
   - B 100 millimetres
   - C 150 millimetres
   - D 200 millimetres

8. There is a major tourist area in the parish of:
   - A St James
   - B St Ann
   - C St Mary
   - D St Thomas

9. The area where the natural environment is not protected is the:
   - A Dry Harbour Mountains
   - B Cockpit Country
   - C Portland Bight
   - D John Crow Mountains

Answers to questions 10 to 13 can be found in the thematic maps of Guyana (**pages 54 and 55**).

10. In which part of Guyana is sugar refined?
    - A south-west
    - B north-west
    - C north-east
    - D south-east

11. The annual rainfall in the area to the south-west of the Kaieteur Falls (B3) is:
    - A over 3,000 millimetres
    - B between 2,500 and 3,000 millimetres
    - C between 1,500 and 2,000 millimetres
    - D under 1,500 millimetres per year

12. The number of towns in Guyana that have a population of between 10,000 and 100,000 is:
    - A three
    - B five
    - C seven
    - D nine

13. The majority of Guyana's land is covered in:
    - A crops and fruit
    - B savannah grazing
    - C forest and woods
    - D urban areas

20 Test on thematic maps

Answers to questions 14 to 17 can be found on **page 82**, which has information on the world's population.

14 How many very large cities in Australia have over ten million people?
- **A** None
- **B** One
- **C** Three
- **D** Five

15 Which of the following cities with populations of over ten million is not in Africa?
- **A** Cairo
- **B** Istanbul
- **C** Kinshasa
- **D** Lagos

16 The world's five largest cities are in:
- **A** Asia
- **B** North America
- **C** South America
- **D** Europe

17 In 2018, the world's population was about:
- **A** 7,600,000,000
- **B** 7,600,000
- **C** 8,000,000
- **D** 39,800,000

The answers to questions 18 to 20 are on the world climate and environment maps (**pages 78 to 80**).

18 The annual rainfall in Lima, Peru, is:
- **A** Mountainous climate
- **B** Hot desert climate
- **C** 45 millimetres
- **D** 20°C

19 The month when average temperature is highest in Quebec, Canada, is:
- **A** June
- **B** July
- **C** August
- **D** September

20 The island of Borneo is:
- **A** covered by tropical rain forest that is being rapidly cut down
- **B** a desert subject to continuous drought
- **C** covered with tropical grassland that is turning into desert due to soil erosion
- **D** an area of tundra vegetation with heavily polluted seas and lakes

PART 4 ACQUIRE PLACE KNOWLEDGE

21 Know your own country

NEW SKILL

Strengthen knowledge and understanding of your own country through application of skills acquired in earlier chapters of this workbook.

Ten exercises are outlined below. They will help you to get to know your country better and allow you to practise skills you have been learning as you worked through this workbook, section by section. It is intended that your class share these exercises in groups of three or four. Every group should use the same outline map of your country.

The online pages for this workbook provide an outline map for all the English-speaking countries of the Caribbean. Find the outline map for your own country at **www.hoddereducation.com/atlasworkbook**. Your teacher will print a copy of this outline map for each group. If all maps use the same scale (same size outline map), the display will look professional when all maps are put on the classroom wall.

Begin by getting into small groups. Each group will be assigned one of the ten exercises. Each group will need one or more copies of the *Caribbean School Atlas*. Your group will discuss how to begin and how to make a quality sketch map. Each group is reminded of the chapter where the relevant new skill was introduced.

When all groups have completed maps – including a title and a key for each one – the collection can be put on display in the classroom. The sketch below suggests what such a display looked like for a class of students in the imaginary island of St Sebastian.

Here are the exercises for the ten groups:

Group 1   Make a map of your country's coastline

Shade the sea around the coastline in light blue and name the estuaries, capes and bays. Estuaries occur where large rivers enter the seas or oceans. Capes are pieces of land that jut out into the sea. Bays are places where the coastline is dented in. This exercise uses skills of interpreting landscape introduced in Chapter 6.

Group 2   Make a map of the topography of your country

Make a physical map of your country. First make a key and insert appropriate tints. Then shade in all parts of the land with the correct tint, guided by the atlas map. Label the hills and mountains. This exercise revises skills introduced in Chapter 6 of this workbook on the use of colour tinting to show elevation.

Group 3   Make a map of the main water features of your country

Draw and name the main rivers and lakes of your country. This exercise revises skills in using symbols for water features learned in Chapter 5.

21 Know your own country

Group 4 Make a chart of distances between main cities and towns of your country

Mark the main towns and cities of your country in the correct places. Then use the line scale to find the distance between pairs of towns and show these in a table beside the map. Show the distances you measure in a table like the example below. This exercise revises the skill of calculating real distance using the scale that was explained in Chapter 8.

Between town A and town B		the distance is:
Example		
Port-of-Spain	Arima	26 km

Group 5 Make a map of the administrative divisions of your country

Name the administrative divisions of your country shown on your outline map. Shade each of the divisions a different colour. Name the main town in each division. This exercise revises skills related to interpretation of administrative boundaries introduced in Chapter 17 of this workbook.

Group 6 Make a map to show the main roads of your country

Draw in the main roads of your country. Decide what kind of pattern it is. This exercise revises skills in the interpretation of landscape introduced in Chapter 6.

Group 7 Make a map of agriculture in your country

Make a map of your country to show where two of the country's crops are grown. Begin by making a key to explain the colours or symbols you will use to show the crops. This exercise revises skills in mapping economic activities from Chapter 18.

Group 8 Make a tourism map for your country

Use symbols to show the places that tourists like to stay and sights they like to see. Remember to explain the symbols in a key. You will find tourism maps for several countries in your *Caribbean School Atlas*. This exercise revises skills introduced in Chapter 18.

Group 9 Draw latitude and longitude coordinates on a map of your country

Draw in lines of latitude and longitude on the outline map of your country and write in the degrees and minutes for each line. Remember to write in either E or W for each line of longitude and either N or S for each line of latitude. This exercise revises skills on finding the position of a place in chapter 4.

Group 10 Find directions between towns

Select at least three important towns of your country other than the capital. Find the direction of the three towns from your country's capital, by making a direction finder. Mark the direction from the capital of each town on your map. This exercise revises skills in stating direction from Chapter 7.

PART 4 ACQUIRE PLACE KNOWLEDGE

22 Know the Caribbean region

 NEW SKILL

Use your *Caribbean School Atlas* and the skills you have acquired to get to know the Caribbean region.

What is the Caribbean region?

There is no fixed definition of the Caribbean region. At its core are the islands of the archipelago, the string of islands that separate the Caribbean Sea from the Atlantic Ocean. Look at the map on atlas **pages 8–9** and find the following places that mark the outer boundaries of the archipelago:
- Cape San Antonio, Cuba, in the west (B2)
- Abaco Island, the Bahamas, to the north (C1)
- Kitridge Point, Barbados, to the east (G4)
- Galeota Point, Trinidad, to the south-east (F4)

Based on the above extreme points, let's get an idea of how large the archipelago is.

1 Measure the distance from Kitridge Point, Barbados, to Cape San Antonio, Cuba (roughly east to west):

   .... km

2 Measure the distance from Abaco Island, the Bahamas, to Galeota Point, Trinidad:

   .... km

The coastline of parts of South America and Central America are on the Caribbean Sea. These areas are shown on the lower map on **page 15**. Belize and the islands of the Netherlands Caribbean (see **page 45**) are considered Caribbean countries.

Also, the three countries on the northern coast of South America, to the east of Venezuela (see **page 63**), are considered Caribbean countries although none is touched by the Caribbean Sea.

3 The names of the three Caribbean countries to the east of Venezuela are:

   ....

   ....

Independent or belonging to another country?

Most countries of the Caribbean region are independent – they rule themselves now, unlike in the past. The lower map on atlas **page 15** gives you the year in which independence was proclaimed. Look for your country on this map and see in which year it became independent.

Other islands still belong to European countries or to the USA. The European countries that still have islands in the Caribbean are France, the Netherlands and the United Kingdom (UK or Britain).

Let's do detective work using your *Caribbean School Atlas* to find islands controlled by European countries and the USA.

4 The Caribbean territories that are part of the USA (clue: see **page 35**) are

   .... and ....

5 The five Caribbean territories that are still governed by the UK are:

   ....

   ....

   ....

(Clue: look in the fact files on **pages 24, 25, 36 and 37** and find the territories that include the British flag, called the Union Jack, in the top left-hand corner of the territory flag. If you do not know what the Union Jack looks like, you can find it on **page 75**!)

6 The two overseas departments of France in the Caribbean (clue: see **page 40**) are

   ....

7 The six islands of the Caribbean Netherlands (clue: see **page 45**) are

   ....

   ....

   ....

   ....

22 Know the Caribbean region

What is the Caribbean Community?

To begin to answer this, let's look again at the maps of the Caribbean region on atlas **page 15**. The top map shows the countries that controlled islands and mainland territories for hundreds of years. Great Britain was one of those countries.

Look at the places marked in orange as once British. How many can you count? These places were until the 1960s part of the British Empire, which stretched across all six continents of the world.

British colonies demanded and fought for their independence. But they had made close ties with Britain and with each other over several centuries, so most of them opted to continue these ties as members of the Commonwealth of Nations. You can find a map of all the current members of the Commonwealth on **page 84**. There were 53 members in 2018.

> The twelve Caribbean members of the Commonwealth are shown in the small map at the centre of **page 84**.
>
> 8 List the twelve Caribbean independent countries that are members of the Commonwealth of Nations.
>
>   ....
>   ....
>   ....
>   ....
>   ....
>   ....
>
> Therefore, when you hear the term Commonwealth Caribbean, these twelve independent countries belong to this group. All use English as their official language.

In addition to these twelve independent Caribbean countries, the term Commonwealth Caribbean also includes the five British Overseas Territories located in the Caribbean. You identified these Question 5.

The Caribbean Community, or CARICOM, was established in 1973 by four independent countries, all former British colonies, to improve the economies of member countries through cooperation. Another eleven countries joined after 1973. And five British Overseas Territories have joined as associate members (not full members, as these are not independent).

> Let's make lists of CARICOM countries in the table overleaf.
>
> 10 Use the map of CARICOM on atlas **page 19** to find the four countries that founded CARICOM in 1973.
>
> 11 Use this map to list eleven other countries that joined CARICOM after 1973.
>
> 12 Use the map on page 19 to list the five British Overseas Territories than are associate members of CARICOM. (This list of five includes one territory that is not in the list you made earlier for Question 5.)
>
> 13 List the two CARICOM members whose official language is not English (you may have to look at the fact files).

PART 4 ACQUIRE PLACE KNOWLEDGE

Question	10	11	12	13
List	Founding members	Other full members	Associate members	Non-English-speaking members
Number of countries	4	11	5	2
Country names	....	....	....	....
	....	....	....	....
	....	....	....	
	....	....	....	
		....	....	
		....		
		....		
		....		
		....		
		....		
		....		

Make your own map

Increase your knowledge of the region in which you live in by creating your own map of the countries of the Caribbean region.

> You will find a double-page outline map of the Caribbean on pages 100-101 of this workbook. The exercise that follows will help you to learn where 40 Caribbean countries are located. Use atlas **pages 10, 11 and 19** to help you to complete the instructions below.
> - Colour green the fifteen countries that are members of CARICOM. You will find them on **page 19** of your atlas.
> - Now write in the name of these fifteen countries in the correct labels on your map. These 15 member-countries include two which are not English speaking.
> - There are five other territories that are associated with CARICOM. These are overseas territories of Britain. Find these small territories and draw a green circle around each one. Bermuda is outside the map, so put a circle nearest to its location, north of the Bahamas. Next, write the names of these five territories in the right spaces.
> - Colour orange all the other countries on the map and write in their names.
> - Finish your map by neatly colouring the sea and ocean in light blue. Do not colour inside the country name labels.
> - Check your map carefully. Make sure you have put the correct country name in each label.
> - Write your name in the space provided.
> - Each label has a number. Your teacher will read out the 40 country names by number. You can check whether you have the correct country named in each label.

Flags of the Commonwealth Caribbean

You learned earlier that the Commonwealth Caribbean comprises twelve independent countries and five British Overseas Territories. Outlines of the flags of these seventeen independent countries and non-independent territories are given in the task box.

22 Know the Caribbean region

⏰ Identify each flag and colour it in carefully. You will find their colours in the fact files of the Caribbean Countries section of your *Caribbean School Atlas*. Write the country name in the space below each flag.

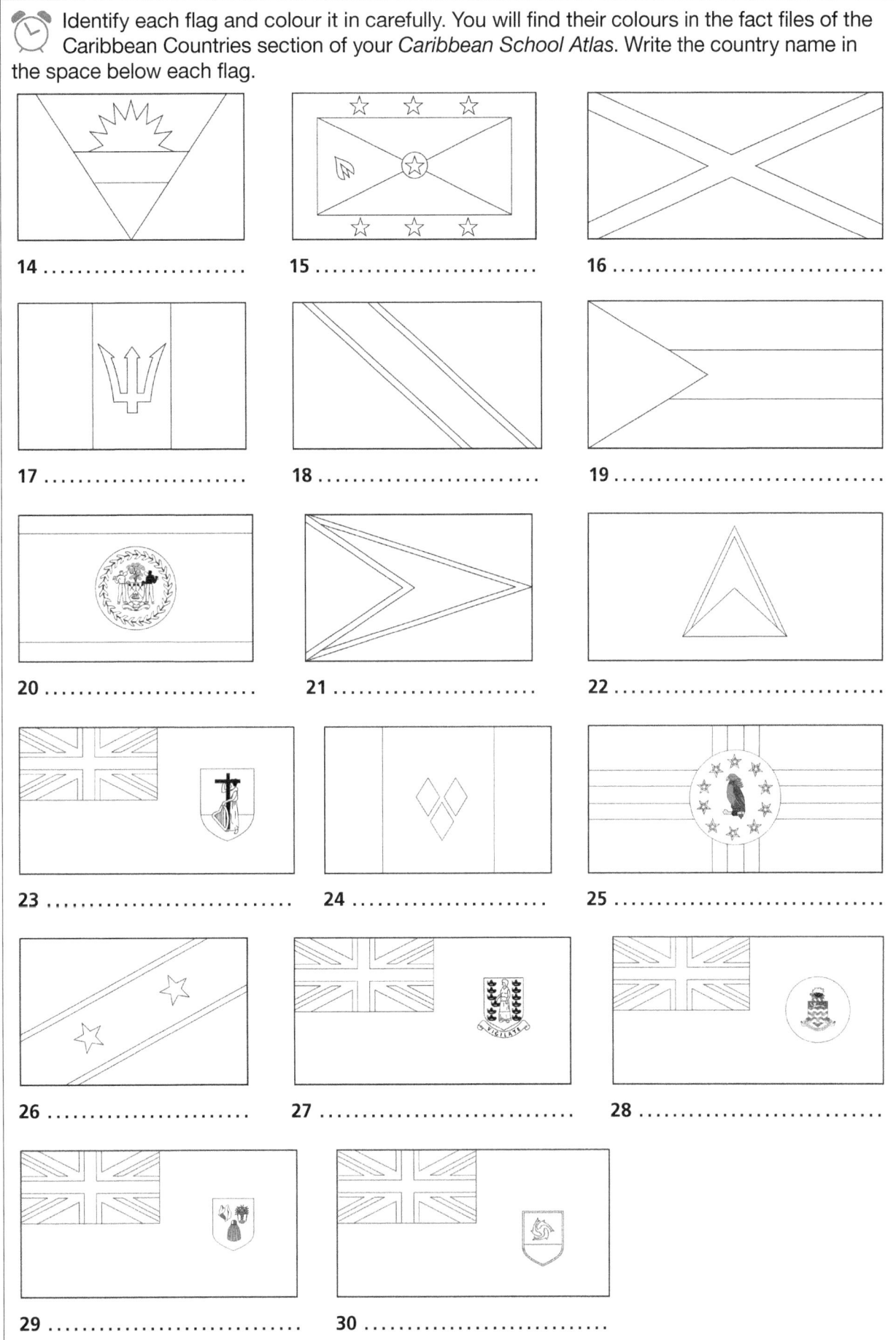

14 .... 15 .... 16 ....

17 .... 18 .... 19 ....

20 .... 21 .... 22 ....

23 .... 24 .... 25 ....

26 .... 27 .... 28 ....

29 .... 30 ....

Flags of Commonwealth Caribbean countries and territories

PART 4 ACQUIRE PLACE KNOWLEDGE

Make a display of maps of Caribbean countries

 Caribbean country outline maps from the web page can be printed and used to learn more about the Caribbean region. Your teacher can make exercises like the ten map-making exercises in Chapter 21.

Each member of your class can make one map for a country, using the outline maps. Your class can make a display of all the maps to celebrate Commonwealth Day or CARICOM Day.

USING THE RIGHT MAPS FOR THE JOB

A small boat with three fishermen left Old Harbour Bay, Jamaica, for a ten-day fishing trip around the Pedro Cays to the south. It has been twenty days since they set off. There was a report that parts of a fishing boat were seen floating off the coast of Belize. Families of the fishermen fear the worst. The Jamaican, Belizean and Honduran coastguards are searching for the missing fishermen.

On the map below, shade the area that you think should be the focus for the search.

Complete this sentence: You recommend that the search area be bounded by latitude .... to the south and latitude .... to the north. The search should also be bounded by longitude .... to the east and longitude .... to the west.

If you were put in charge of the search, how would you organise all the coastguard boats to look for the missing men? Show your search plan on the map.

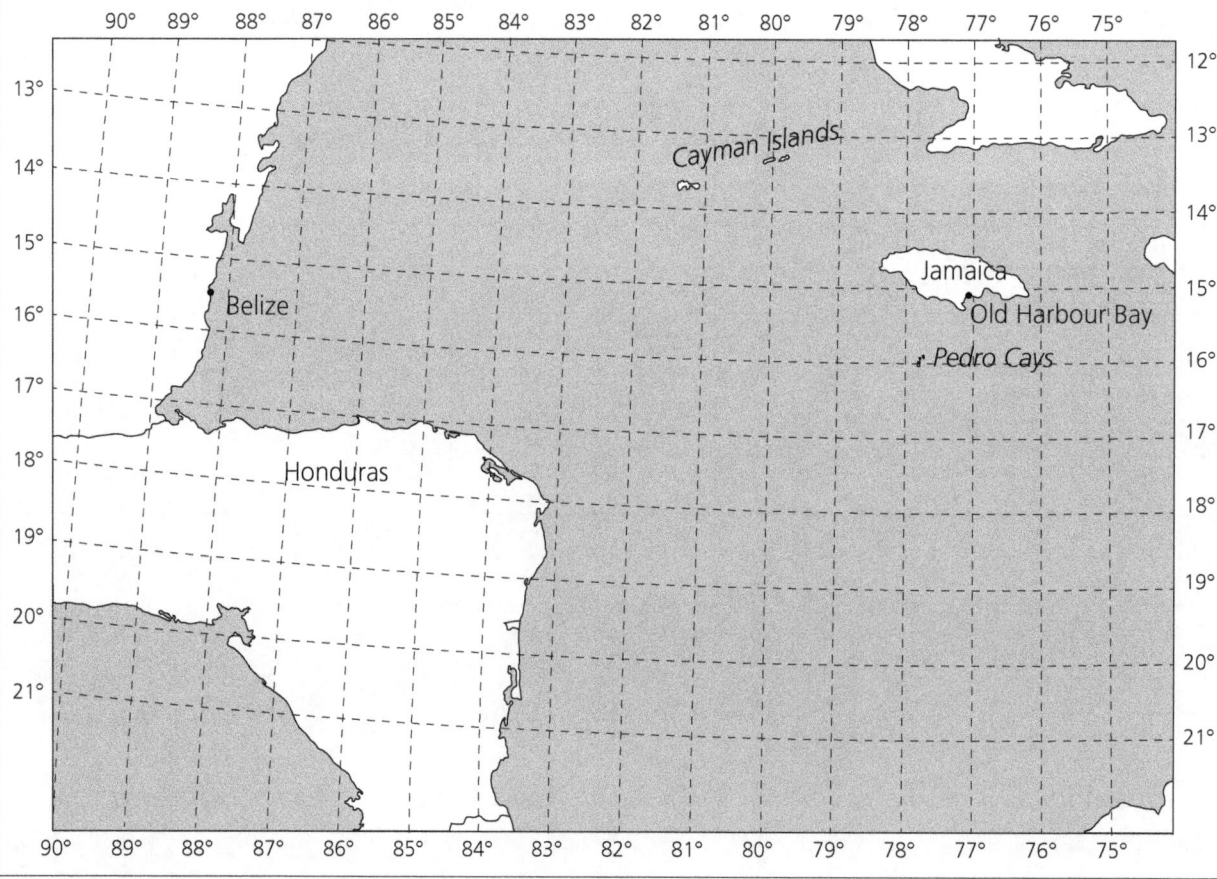

QQ Quick quiz about the Caribbean

Select the correct response for these quiz questions about the Caribbean region. Tick a, b, c or d.

1. The Caribbean region includes:
   - a Belize and Guyana
   - b Bermuda and Brazil
   - c Peru and Ecuador
   - d Brazil and Mexico

2. This country is not in the Commonwealth Caribbean:
   - a Guyana
   - b Cayman Islands
   - c Jamaica
   - d Haiti

3. CARICOM comprises:
   - a the Caribbean region
   - b fifteen members and five associate members
   - c the Caribbean territories of Britain, the Netherlands and France
   - d only former countries of the British Empire

4. The Caribbean country with the largest population is:
   - a Cuba
   - b Jamaica
   - c Haiti
   - d Barbados

5. Below is the outline of the flag of:
   - a St Lucia
   - b Guyana
   - c Trinidad and Tobago
   - d Antigua and Barbuda

23 Know your world

 NEW SKILL

Increase your knowledge of the world. Utilise your *Caribbean School Atlas* to acquire place vocabulary – a mental map of the physical and human patterns of the world in which we live. Patterns include knowledge of continents, oceans, seas, countries and cities.

Continents

Look at the world map on atlas **pages 56 and 57**. You can see the seven large landmasses of the world called continents. The continent names are printed in bold letters. Make use of this double-page map and touch the places on the map as you read the facts in the list:

- The size of each continent is stated in the fact file below the map. Continents are listed in order of size in thousands of square kilometres. Asia is the largest. Australia is the smallest.
- Antarctica is distorted and partly hidden on **pages 56 and 57**. This is because of the way the spherical Earth has been projected on a flat sheet of paper. There is a better map of Antarctica on **page 72**. It is almost entirely inside the Antarctic Circle, with the South Pole at its centre.
- The Australian continent is larger than Australia the country. As a continent, its land area includes the island of New Guinea to its north. Look for Australia in the Continents and Countries Facts & Figures on **page 75**.

PART 4 ACQUIRE PLACE KNOWLEDGE

- Antarctica and Australia are not joined to any other continent.
- Africa is joined to Asia by land that lies between the Red Sea and the Mediterranean Sea.
- North America is joined to South America by a narrow strip of land called an isthmus. The country called Panama lies along the isthmus and is the location of the Panama Canal.
- Europe and Asia are joined together. The boundary between Europe and Asia exists on paper. There is no significant physical distinction between the two continents.
- The boundary between Europe and Asia is a construct of human history and culture. The boundary between Asia and Europe is defined as (1) beginning in the Aegean Sea, between Greece and Turkey; (2) passing through the Turkish Strait to the Black Sea; (3) flowing through the Caucasus mountains to the Caspian Sea; and then (4) following the Ural river and Ural Mountains. Follow this boundary on the map of Europe on atlas **page 66**.
- Many countries straddle the continents of Europe and Asia. These include Turkey, Russia, Kazakhstan, Georgia and Azerbaijan.

You should be able to recognise the shapes of the continents. Look at the shapes of the continents in your atlas. When you think you can recognise each one, download the Continents challenge sheet from the online map bank.

The shapes are the outlines of the continents, excluding Antarctica, but arranged randomly. Try to remember them without checking in your atlas. Write the names of these six continents on the labels numbered 1–6.

Next, cut out the shapes along the dotted lines. Then take an A4 piece of card or paper and organise the shapes on it. Move them around until you get all six in the correct positions and then glue them in place. When you have finished shade the continents on your map different colours. The maps from your class can then be used to make a bright display for your classroom.

Let's revise what we have learned about continents. Select the correct word or words to complete the following sentences.

1 .... is the second largest of the seven continents. (Antarctica, Africa, Australia)

2 The area of Australia the country is .... square kilometres. (8,557,000 or 8,557 or 7,741,220)

3 The country Australia together with the island of .... comprise the Australian continent. (New Guinea, Papua New Guinea, New Guinea island)

4 The boundary between Europe and Asia is .... (an ocean, human-constructed, a Great Wall)

Countries of the world

All the independent countries of the world are listed on atlas **pages 73 to 75**. Count the number of countries in each continent. Then add these numbers together to find the number of countries listed on these atlas pages.

Continent	Number of countries listed in atlas	Total number of countries in the world
North America		
South America		
Africa		
Asia		
Australia and the Pacific Ocean		
Europe		
Antarctica		

This number changes all the time as new countries are created. This list was correct in June 2018, but it may be different in a subsequent year. New countries are formed when a country breaks up (Sudan became two countries in 2011). New countries also form when existing countries merge (East Germany and West Germany joined together in 1990).

23 Know your world

North America

Let's get to know the countries of North America. Look at the map of North America on atlas **page 61**. You will find that Caribbean countries are listed as part of North America on **page 73**, but as we have already learned about the Caribbean region elsewhere in this workbook, it is not included in these exercises.

The North American mainland is divided into ten separate countries. Seven of these are grouped together as Central America – the list is below the map.

The United States of America (also known as the USA or the US) occupies two different parts of the continent, although it is a single country. Alaska, in the north-west of North America, is one of the 50 states that comprise the USA. There is one state in the Pacific (Hawaii) and many other territories, such as Puerto Rico and the United States Virgin Islands in the Caribbean, which are not fully incorporated into the country. Do you know the names of some of the other 48 states?

> The countries of mainland North America and the large island to its north-east are numbered 1 to 11 on the outline map of the continent on page 95 of this workbook. The largest countries of North America are numbered 1 to 3. The seven countries of Central America are numbered 4 to 10. The island, labelled 11, belongs to a European country.
>
> Your tasks:
> - Fill in the names of the eleven countries, referring to **page 61** of your *Caribbean School Atlas*.
> - Look at the physical map of North America on **page 60** and find the names of the two major mountain ranges marked 12 and 13 on the outline map. Label these two ranges on your map.
> - Make a languages map. The official language of each country is given below. Shade in the key first. Then colour each country according to its official language.
>
> | Canada uses English and French. | Greenland uses Danish. |
> |---|---|
> | USA and Belize use English. | The other eight countries of North America use Spanish. |
>
> - Give your map an appropriate title.

South America

> Let's get to know the countries of South America. Look at the two maps of South America on atlas **pages 62 and 63**. Then use the outline map of South America on page 98 to complete this exercise.
>
> Your tasks:
> - Begin by writing in the names of the countries.
> - Next, shade in the key with five colours, one for each of the official languages used in South American countries. Brazil uses Portuguese, Guyana uses English, Suriname uses Dutch, French Guiana uses French. The other nine countries use Spanish. Colour the countries appropriately.
> - Name the important mountain range, parts of which are in seven South American countries.
> - Give your map an appropriate title.

Europe

Let's get to know the countries of Europe. There are many countries in Europe. Some are very large, such as Germany. Some are very small, such as Luxembourg. Look at atlas **page 67** and see how many country names you already know.

A total of 28 European countries have joined the European Union (EU). See **page 85** of your atlas to see when each one joined. Trade and movement of people between these countries are free. Countries wish to join or leave, so the number of members may change in the future.

> The EU countries are numbered 1 to 28 on the outline map of Europe on page 97 of this workbook.
>
> Your tasks:
> - Write in the names of the 28 EU member countries on the outline map.
> - Shade in blue all the member countries of the EU on the outline map. Remember to shade the key first. Blue is the special colour of the EU.
> - There are many other important European countries that have not joined the EU. Examples are numbered 29–35 on the outline map. Find their names and write them in – but do not shade these countries blue!
> - Give your map a title.

PART 4 ACQUIRE PLACE KNOWLEDGE

Africa

⏰ Let's get to know the countries of Africa. Look at the two maps of Africa on atlas **pages 64 and 65**. There are 55 African countries. These are listed on atlas **pages 73 and 74** with facts and figures for each country.

Let's find out which parts of Africa were the homelands of millions of Africans enslaved and transported to the Caribbean over many centuries. The map below shows where Africans were captured.

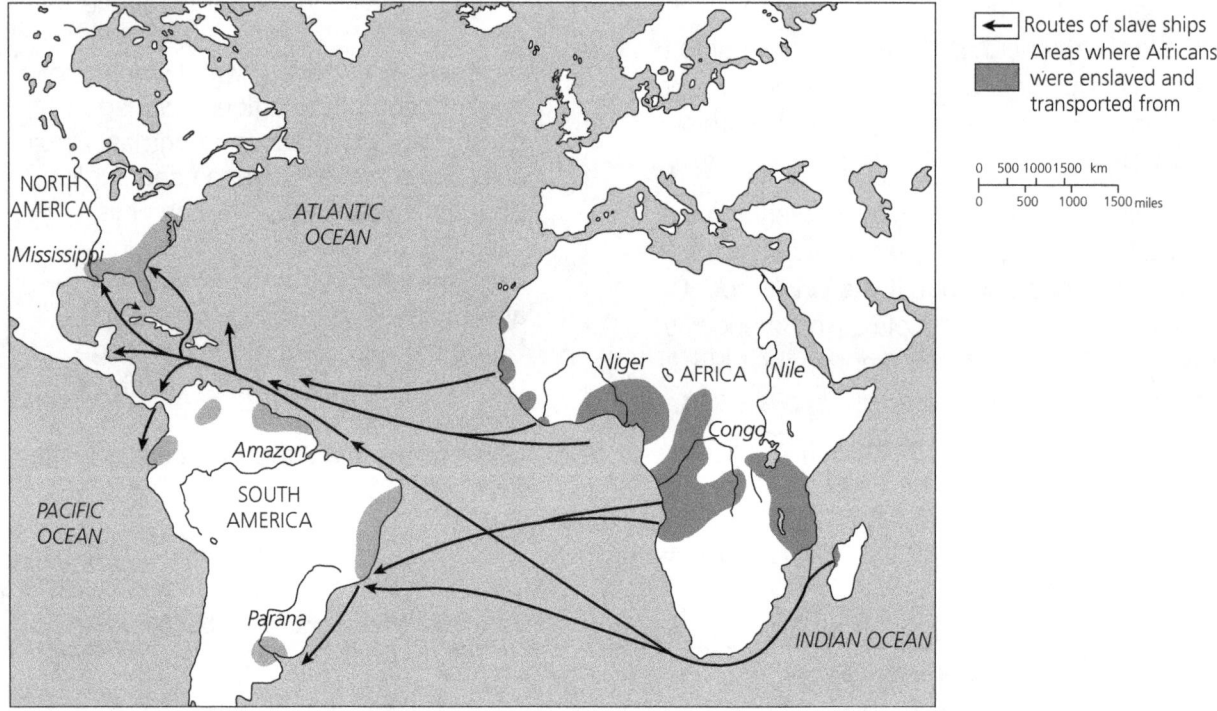

Homelands of Africans enslaved and transported to the Caribbean and the Americas

Your tasks:
- Eighteen African countries are numbered on the outline map on page 102 of this workbook. Find the name of each country numbered and write its name in the correct box.
- Africans were enslaved and transported to the Caribbean in large numbers from places in western, south-western and south-eastern Africa. Tint the key in a colour to show the areas of origin of enslaved Africans.
- Now copy the shaded areas from the above map onto your map of the African continent.
- Make a list of ten of the present-day countries of Africa that were in the past the source of enslaved people who were sent to the Caribbean in slave ships.

Present-day African countries which were the source of forced migration for peoples of the Caribbean today	

Asia

Let's get to know some of the major countries of Asia. Look at the maps of Asia on atlas **pages 68 and 69**. There is an outline map of Asia online. You should print this and use it to complete the following tasks.

Your tasks:
- Fifteen countries are numbered on the outline map. Find these and name them.
- Over the past 150 years, people have migrated from four parts of Asia and settled in the Caribbean. They came from north-eastern parts of India, south-eastern parts of China, Syria and Lebanon, and Java in present-day Indonesia. Shade each of these areas on your map of Asia with a different colour tint and create a key.
- There are two great mountain ranges marked 16 and 17 on the outline map. Look for their names on atlas **page 68** and name them on the outline map.

Finally, look for some of the great rivers of Asia and complete these sentences.

5 The .... river rises in the Himalayas and flows through India and Bangladesh into the Bay of Bengal.

6 The longest river in China is the .... It flows into the Yellow Sea near Shanghai.

7 The Mekong River rises in the Himalayas and flows south through several countries (Ch..............., La..............., Ca............... and V...............), before flowing into the South China Sea near Ho Chi Minh City.

8 The main river that flows through Pakistan is the ....

Australia and the Pacific

Let's get to know the countries of the Australian continent and the Pacific region. Together, these are sometimes referred to Oceania or Australasia.

Study the maps on atlas **pages 70 and 71** and complete the following sentences about Australia and the Pacific.

9 The mountain range along Australia's eastern coastline is called the ....

10 The peak of Mount Kosciuszko, the highest point in Australia, is .... metres.

11 The largest coral barrier reef in the world (see E3 and F4 and the satellite photograph on **page 71**) is the ....

12 To the east of Australia is the .... Ocean.

13 To the west of Australia is the .... Ocean.

14 The Tasman Sea is between Australia and ....

15 Tasmania is in the .... Ocean.

16 The western half of the island of New Guinea is part of ....

17 The country New Zealand consists of the islands of .... and ....

18 Name the three European and North American countries that still control groups of Pacific Islands.

....

....

PART 4 ACQUIRE PLACE KNOWLEDGE

Four of the countries of the Australian continent and the Pacific Ocean are numbered 1 to 4 on the online outline map. Print a copy. Find the name of each country numbered and write it in the space provided next to the correct number.

Learn the names of the other countries by writing their names neatly on the map.

The Pacific and the Caribbean are linked! Breadfruit and other Pacific Ocean fruits were transported to St Vincent and Jamaica from the island of Tahiti in 1793 in a special expedition commanded by Captain Bligh. Find Tahiti and Jamaica on the map on atlas **page 70**.

Bligh's convoy couldn't head east to Jamaica as there was no Panama Canal at the time. Instead, Bligh navigated westward. He stopped at Timor (in present-day Indonesia), passed the Cape of Good Hope, and made further stops at St Helena and St Vincent on the way to Jamaica.

19 Use the world map on atlas **pages 56 and 57** to find the route Bligh followed and then estimate the length of his voyage from Tahiti to Jamaica. .... kilometres

---

The world's capitals

Let's discover how to find the name of a country's capital! There are two ways. First, the world Facts & Figures table of your atlas (pages 73–75) lists every independent country and its capital. Second, on all atlas maps a country's capital is underlined.

Name the capital of the following countries. You can use the world Facts & Figures on **pages 73 to 75** to find the names.

20 Zimbabwe ....

21 India ....

22 China ....

23 Slovakia ....

24 Uruguay ....

25 Nicaragua ....

26 Papua New Guinea ....

27 Haiti ....

Here are some capitals. Name the countries they are in. You can use the index and the atlas maps to find the country.

28 Brasilia ....

29 Paramaribo ....

30 Jakarta ....

31 Tripoli ....

32 Kiev ....

33 A capital can be a large city or a small town, depending on the population of the country itself. Here are five capitals: a) Bangkok, b) Basseterre, c) Belmopan, d) Berlin and e) Brasilia. Use information in your atlas to put them in order, from largest to smallest.

Largest				Smallest

Oceans, seas and lakes

Let's get to know the oceans, seas and lakes of the world!
You have been learning about the world's land areas. But they take up only about 30 per cent of the Earth's surface. Oceans and seas cover 70 per cent.

> Look again at the world map on atlas **pages 56 and 57**. This time focus on the areas coloured blue – the oceans, seas and lakes. Four of the world's oceans are numbered 1 to 4 on the outline map overleaf. Find them in your atlas and write the ocean names on the outline map.

> Just as the continents are divided into countries and regions, there are names for different parts of oceans. These parts may be called sea, bay, gulf, strait or basin. Some are named on the physical maps in your atlas. Look for the names of those numbered 5 to 10 on the outline map on the next page and complete the following sentences.

34 The .... Sea is separated from the Atlantic Ocean by the Caribbean archipelago.

35 The Mississippi river flows into the Gulf of .... at New Orleans.

36 Between Great Britain and Norway/Denmark is the .... Sea.

37 The .... Sea is linked to the Atlantic Ocean by the Strait of Gibraltar.

38 The Gulf of .... is part of the Atlantic Ocean bordering West Africa.

39 The Bay of .... is surrounded on three sides by India, Bangladesh and Myanmar.

Now complete these sentences about the location of oceans in relation to continents, referring to numbers 1 to 4 on the outline map.

40 The Atlantic Ocean is between the continents of North America and ....

   to its west, and Europe and .... to its east.

41 Africa, Asia and Australia border the .... Ocean.

42 The Pacific Ocean lies between three continents: ....

   ....

   ....

43 The .... Ocean is to the north of Europe, Asia and North America.

Finally, let's get to know some of the world's giant water bodies that lie within continents. Most are completely surrounded by land. Some are called seas, some lakes. Use your atlas to find the water bodies marked 48 to 53 on the outline map on page 97 of this workbook.

44 ....   47 ....

45 ....   48 ....

46 ....   49 ....

PART 4 ACQUIRE PLACE KNOWLEDGE

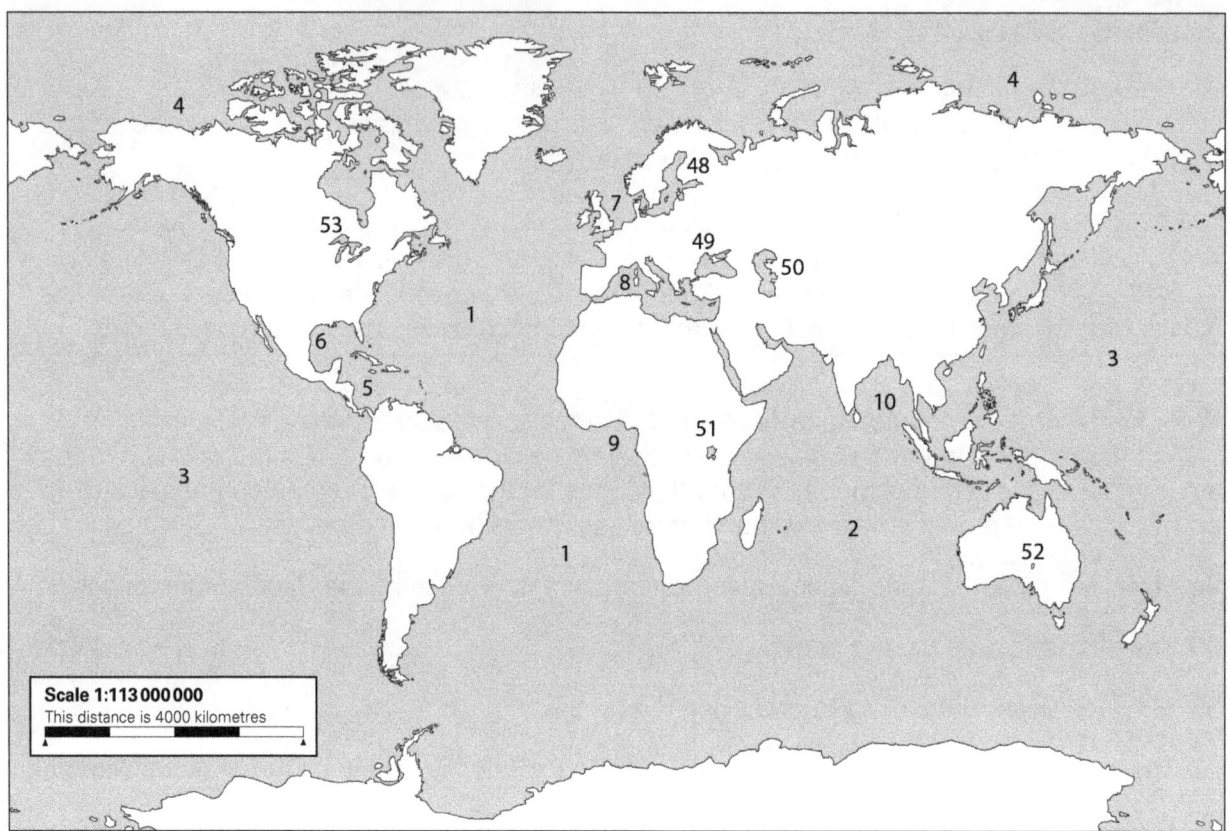

Earth as a planet of the solar system

Finally, let's find out where planet Earth fits into the universe. Planet Earth, called 'the world' by we who live on it, is one of the planets of the solar system. Use atlas **pages 76 and 77** to insert words from the left-hand column into the correct space in the sentences on the right.

anticlockwise galaxies planets satellite seven Sun 27 365 Equator Moon rotates seasons stars 23.5 150 24	50 The universe is made of many .... 51 The Sun is one of the .... in the galaxy called the Milky Way. 52 Earth is one of the Sun's .... and is .... million kilometres from the Sun. 53 As well as Earth, another .... planets revolve around the Sun. 54 Earth takes .... days to complete one orbit around the Sun. 55 When viewed from above the North Pole, Earth revolves around the Sun in an .... direction. 56 Earth also .... on its axis once in every .... hours. 57 Earth is tilted at .... degrees and, as a result, those places far from the .... experience four .... each year. 58 The only source of heat and light for planet Earth is the .... 59 The Earth has one .... of its own. We call it the .... It takes .... days to orbit Earth.

23 Know your world

QQ Quick quiz about our world

You can use your *Caribbean School Atlas* to find answers to this quiz. Select the correct answer. Tick a, b, c or d.

1. Which of the following statements is correct?
   a. The world has six continents
   b. Asia is joined to Europe and Africa
   c. Australia is the largest continent by area
   d. North and South America are joined by an isthmus

2. The continent that is not divided into countries is:
   a. Antarctica
   b. Australia
   c. Africa
   d. Asia

3. Which of the following is not an ocean?
   a. Pacific
   b. Indian
   c. Southern
   d. Baltic

4. The capital of Russia is:
   a. Kiev
   b. Moscow
   c. Washington
   d. Prague

5. Earth revolves around the Sun in:
   a. 24 hours
   b. 27 days
   c. 150 kilometres
   d. 365 days

24 GAME BOX: KNOWLEDGE OF PLACES

 SKILLS PRACTICE

Try these six activities and have fun practising the skills you have acquired. The games cover: shape recognition, and knowledge of the Caribbean and the world.

Discover sources of two of the world's great rivers

For the two great rivers of the world named below, trace back from the mouth of each one to its several source rivers and list the names of the countries where the source rivers rise. The two rivers are the Amazon and the Nile (**pages 62 and 64**).

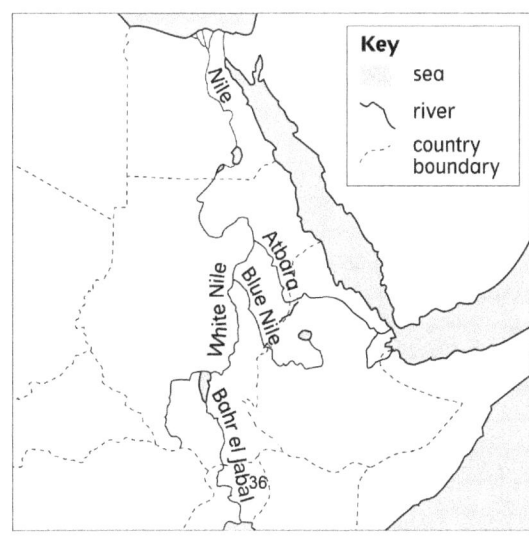

Recognise islands by their shapes

Imagine you are in a spacecraft looking down at the archipelago of Caribbean islands. You would notice that each island has its own distinctive shape. You should be able to recognise Caribbean islands from their shapes.

There are 16 shapes below. The islands are drawn at various scales to fit on the page.

Work through atlas **pages 23 to 55** and discover the name of every island shown in silhouette. Remember – it is the name of the island, not the country! Write the name of each island in the space below its shape.

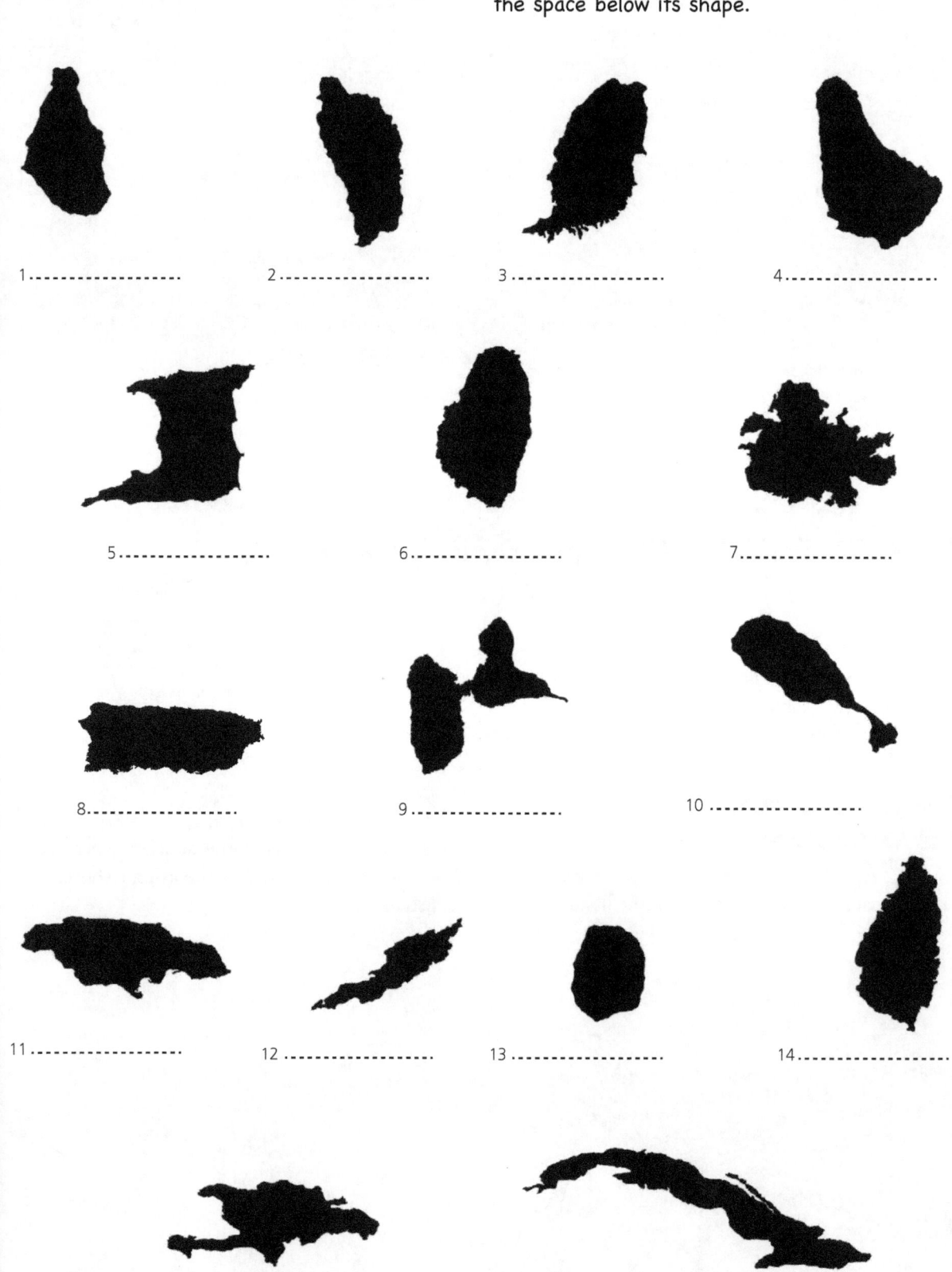

Join the dots; find a Caribbean island

17 This shape looks like the island of

....

Spot errors in flags

18 These are the flags of the four Windward Islands (pages 41 to 44). But three flags have errors. Which flag outline is correct?

....

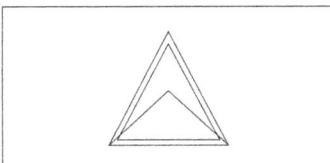
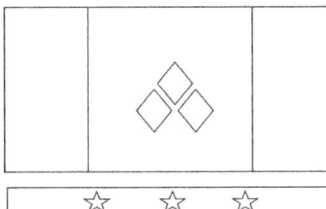
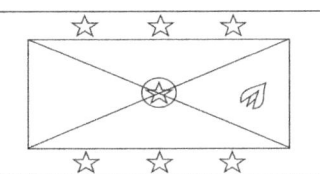

Find ten CARICOM capital cities

Write in the capital city of each of these ten countries in the crossword. Here are the countries:

ACROSS	DOWN	UP
19 Guyana	21 Suriname	26 Grenada
20 Belize	23 Antigua and Barbuda	27 Jamaica
22 Dominica	24 The Bahamas	
25 Trinidad and Tobago		
28 St Vincent and the Grenadines		

What is the population of the Greater Antilles?

29 The Greater Antilles comprises the four largest islands of the Caribbean archipelago. Use the fact files for each of the five countries of the Greater Antilles listed in the table below. Fill in the estimated population for each country. Then add the five populations to calculate the total.

Country	Population
Cuba	
Dominican Republic	
Haiti	
Puerto Rico	
Jamaica	
Greater Antilles total	

Make posters to attract tourists

Imagine you work in the marketing department of a Caribbean travel agency. Use information in the climate graphs on atlas page 78 to create two advertisements to attract Caribbean tourists: one poster for the Mediterranean region of Europe and Africa; and one for Anchorage, Alaska.

Your posters must make it clear why Caribbean countries are targeted. Each poster must refer to:

- the time of year when visitors are encouraged to travel and stay
- activities available in each location that relate to that time of year.

25 Place knowledge tests

SKILLS ASSESSMENT

These tests will help you check your skills in using an atlas to find information.

Caribbean knowledge

Use the Caribbean sections of your *Caribbean School Atlas* (**pages 8 to 55**) to find the correct answer. Only one of the four possible answers given is correct. Tick either A, B, C or D.

1 What name covers four islands: Cuba, Jamaica, Hispaniola (Haiti and Dominican Republic) and Puerto Rico?

- **A** Greater Antilles
- **B** Lesser Antilles
- **C** Leeward Islands
- **D** Windward Islands

2 The official language of Guadeloupe is:

- **A** Dutch
- **B** French
- **C** Portuguese
- **D** Spanish

3 One country that does not belong to CARICOM is:

- **A** Haiti
- **B** Jamaica
- **C** Martinique
- **D** Suriname

4 Between 1500 and 1870 the number of Africans forcibly transported to the Caribbean was:

- **A** under 1 million
- **B** under 3 million
- **C** over 4 million
- **D** over 10 million

5 The two-island country that has a flag with two stars is:

- **A** Antigua and Barbuda
- **B** St Kitts and Nevis
- **C** St Vincent and the Grenadines
- **D** Trinidad and Tobago

6 St George's is the capital of:

- **A** the Bahamas
- **B** Grenada
- **C** Guyana
- **D** Cayman Islands

25 Place knowledge tests

7 The Caribbean country with an estimated population of 180,000 in 2018 is:
- **A** St Lucia
- **B** Barbados
- **C** Dominica
- **D** Montserrat

8 Which of the following eastern Caribbean countries has the largest total land area?
- **A** Dominica
- **B** Grenada
- **C** St Kitts and Nevis
- **D** St Vincent and the Grenadines

9 The total number of visitors landing in Trinidad and Tobago in 2016 was around:
- **A** 40,000
- **B** 500,000
- **C** 1,000,000
- **D** 1,500,000

10 Taino settlements in Jamaica when Europeans arrived in the fifteenth century were mainly:
- **A** distributed around the coast
- **B** located in mountainous areas
- **C** in the area called Portland today
- **D** found in the west of the island

11 None of the Caribbean's major hurricanes between 2004 and 2017 moved in a:
- **A** northerly direction
- **B** north-easterly direction
- **C** north-westerly direction
- **D** south-westerly direction

12 The hurricane that formed in the southern Caribbean off the coast of Columbia in 2012 and moved in a northerly direction was named:
- **A** Wilma
- **B** Matthew
- **C** Katrina
- **D** Sandy

13 Clouds in a hurricane can spiral upward as far as:
- **A** 10 metres
- **B** 100 metres
- **C** 2 kilometres
- **D** 12 kilometres

14 The trend of oil production in Trinidad and Tobago between 2006 and 2016 was:
- **A** declining
- **B** increasing
- **C** same each year
- **D** up and down

15 The photograph on atlas **page 42** was selected to demonstrate:
- **A** the importance of agriculture
- **B** the number of stopover tourists
- **C** the number of cruise passengers
- **D** the topography of the island

16 The district of Belize where coastal areas receive over 4,000 millimetres of rain annually is:
- **A** Belize
- **B** Orange Walk
- **C** Stann Creek
- **D** Toledo

17 This country is not a member state of the OECS:
- **A** Barbados
- **B** Dominica
- **C** St Lucia
- **D** Grenada

18 Which important crop of Grenada is represented in its national flag?
- **A** Bananas
- **B** Cocoa
- **C** Nutmeg
- **D** Vegetables

19 Guyana does not share a border with:
- **A** Trinidad and Tobago
- **B** Suriname
- **C** Brazil
- **D** Venezuela

20 The CARICOM country where Spanish is one of the languages is:
- **A** Panama
- **B** Jamaica
- **C** Suriname
- **D** Belize

World knowledge

Use your *Caribbean School Atlas* to find the correct answer. The focus of the test is knowledge of the world covered in the Continents & Countries section and the World Data section, **pages 56–85**. Only one of the four possible answers given is correct. Tick either A, B, C or D.

21 How many continents are there?
- **A** Four
- **B** Five
- **C** Six
- **D** Seven

22 Which is the largest continent?
- **A** Africa
- **B** Asia
- **C** Europe
- **D** North America

PART 4 ACQUIRE PLACE KNOWLEDGE

23 Which two continents meet at the Ural Mountains?
   A Europe and Asia
   B Asia and Africa
   C North America and South America
   D Europe and Africa

24 Peru is a country of:
   A North America
   B South America
   C Africa
   D Asia

25 Which of these countries does not straddle two continents?
   A Russia   C Italy
   B Turkey   D New Guinea

26 New Zealand is in:
   A Antarctica   C Australia
   B Asia   D the Pacific

27 The ocean to the north of Russia is the:
   A Arctic   C Atlantic
   B Antarctic   D Pacific

28 Between Japan and Canada is the:
   A Arctic Ocean
   B Atlantic Ocean
   C Pacific Ocean
   D Indian Ocean

29 The water body at 60°N 170°E is the:
   A Baring Strait
   B Bering Sea
   C Sea of Okhotsk
   D South China Sea

30 The indentation of an ocean at 00° 00° is named:
   A Gulf of Aden   C Gulf of Guinea
   B Gulf of Mexico   D Gulf of Paria

31 The world's highest mountain range is in:
   A Asia   C North America
   B Europe   D South America

32 The deepest ocean trench is in the:
   A Pacific Ocean
   B Atlantic Ocean
   C Southern Ocean
   D Indian Ocean

33 Of the world's ten longest rivers, how many are in Asia?
   A Three   C Six
   B Four   D Seven

34 Which country is a member state of the European Union (EU)?
   A Turkey   C Switzerland
   B Norway   D Portugal

35 The capital of Mozambique is:
   A Zambezi   C Lilongwe
   B Harare   D Maputo

36 The capital of China is:
   A Hong Kong   C Taipei
   B Beijing   D Taiwan

37 Which of these countries is in West Africa?
   A Tanzania   C Malawi
   B Zimbabwe   D Ghana

38 Day and night are caused by:
   A Earth's revolution around the Sun
   B Earth's rotation on its axis
   C the Moon's revolution around Earth
   D the tilt of the Earth's axis

39 Seasons in countries outside the tropics follow the sequence:
   A Winter, summer, spring, autumn
   B Spring, winter, summer, autumn
   C Summer, spring, winter, autumn
   D Winter, spring, summer, autumn

40 If you were on an expedition in Antarctica on 21 December, the number of hours of sunlight on that date would be:
   A 24   C 12
   B 13.5   D 10.5

SELECTED OUTLINE MAPS

North America

SELECTED OUTLINE MAPS

South America

1 ....
2 ....
3 ....
4 ....
5 ....
6 ....
7 ....
8 ....
9 ....
10 ....
11 ....
12 ....
13 ....
14 The great mountain range is ....

Key
☐ Important mountain range

The official languages of South America:
☐ ....
☐ ....
☐ ....
☐ ....
☐ ....

Scale 1:60 000 000
This distance is 2000 kilometres

SELECTED OUTLINE MAPS

Europe

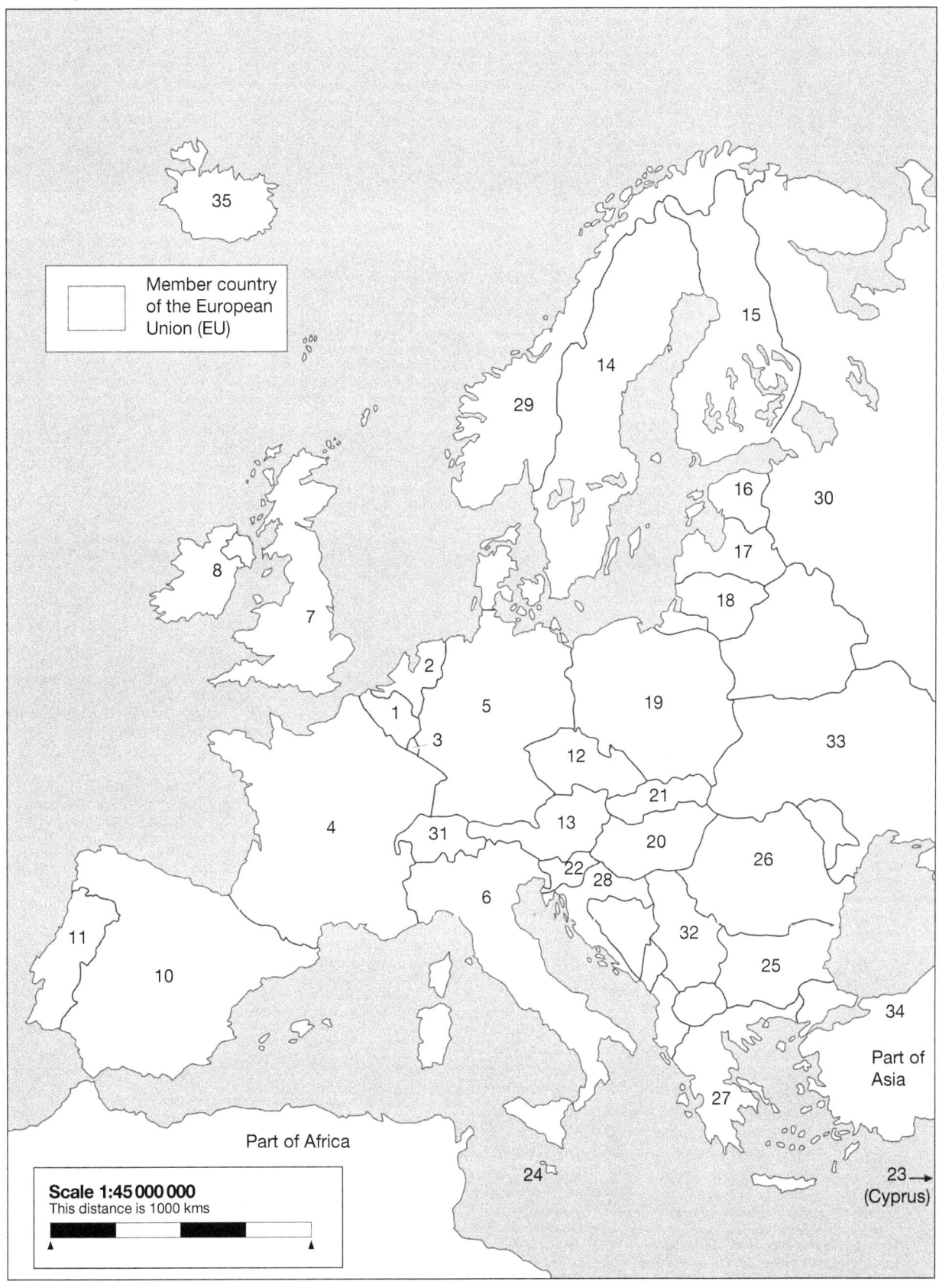

SELECTED OUTLINE MAPS

Caribbean countries

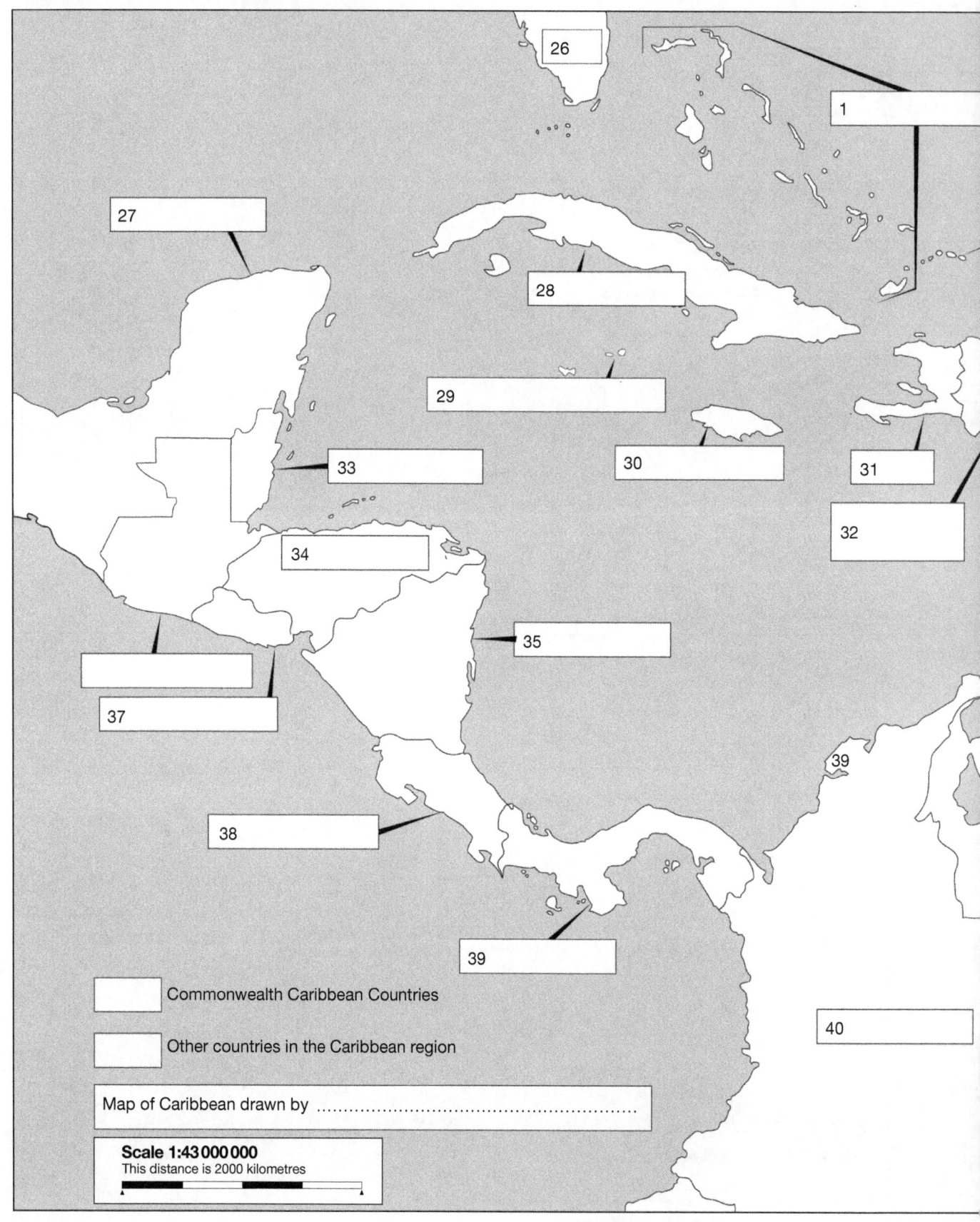

SELECTED OUTLINE MAPS

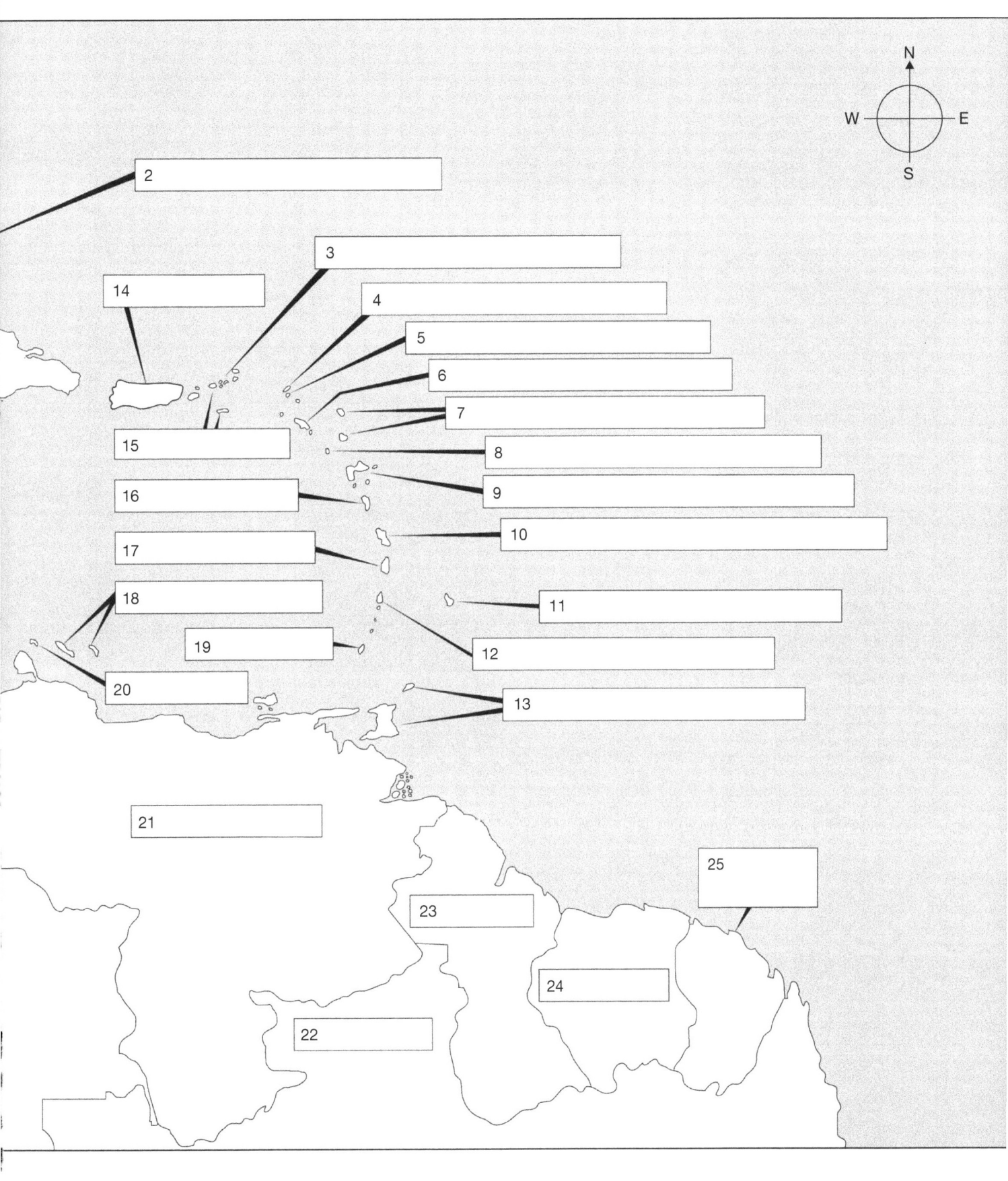

SELECTED OUTLINE MAPS

Caribbean hurricane tracker chart

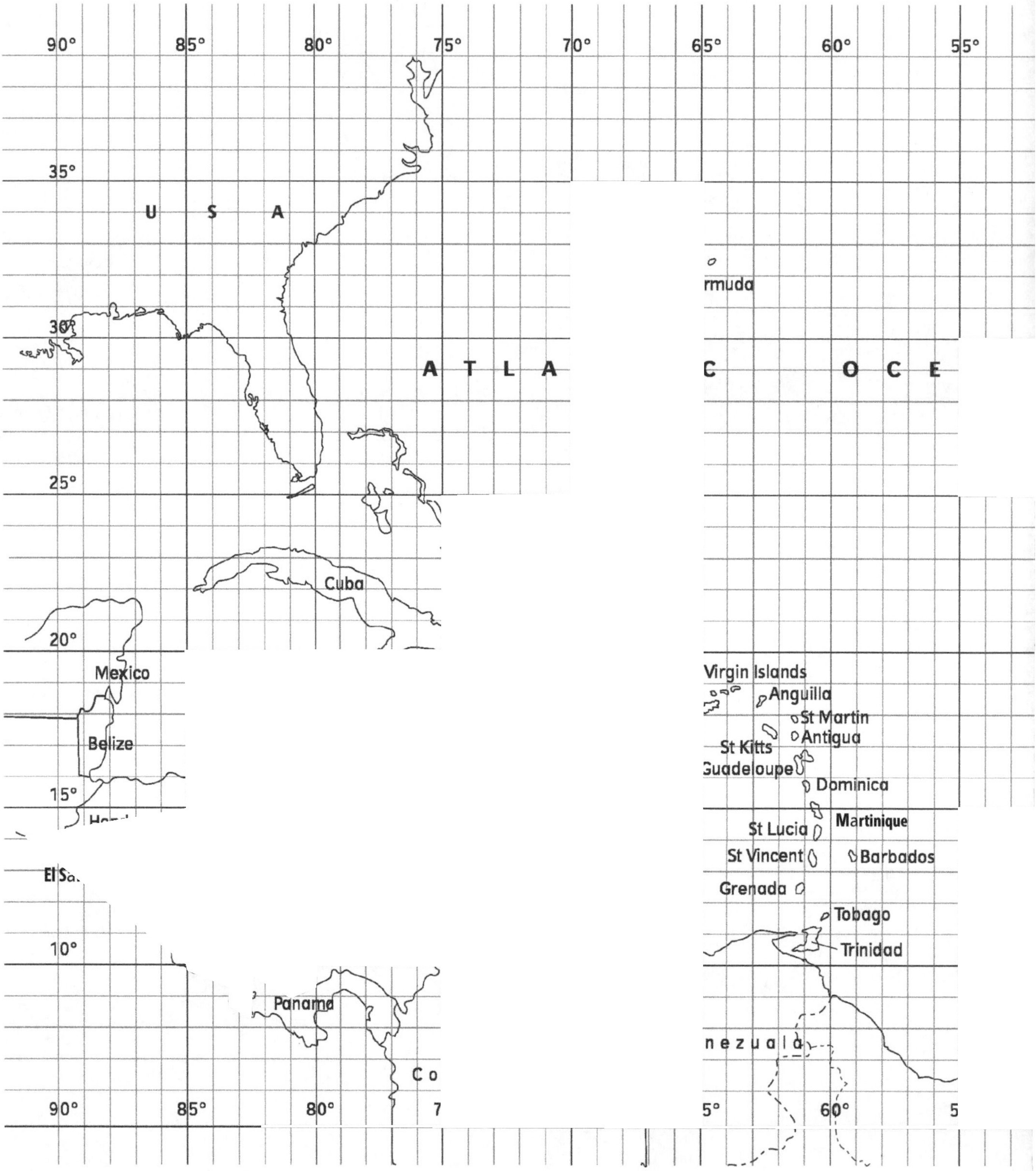

SELECTED OUTLINE MAPS

101

My daily observations log

Storm/hurricane name:

No.	Date	Day of the week	Position latitude	Position longitude	Wind speed	Countries affected
1						
2						
3						
4						
5						
6						
7						
8						
9						
10						
11						
12						

Scale 1:37 000 000
This distance is 1500 kilometres

AFRICA

102 SELECTED OUTLINE MAPS

Africa

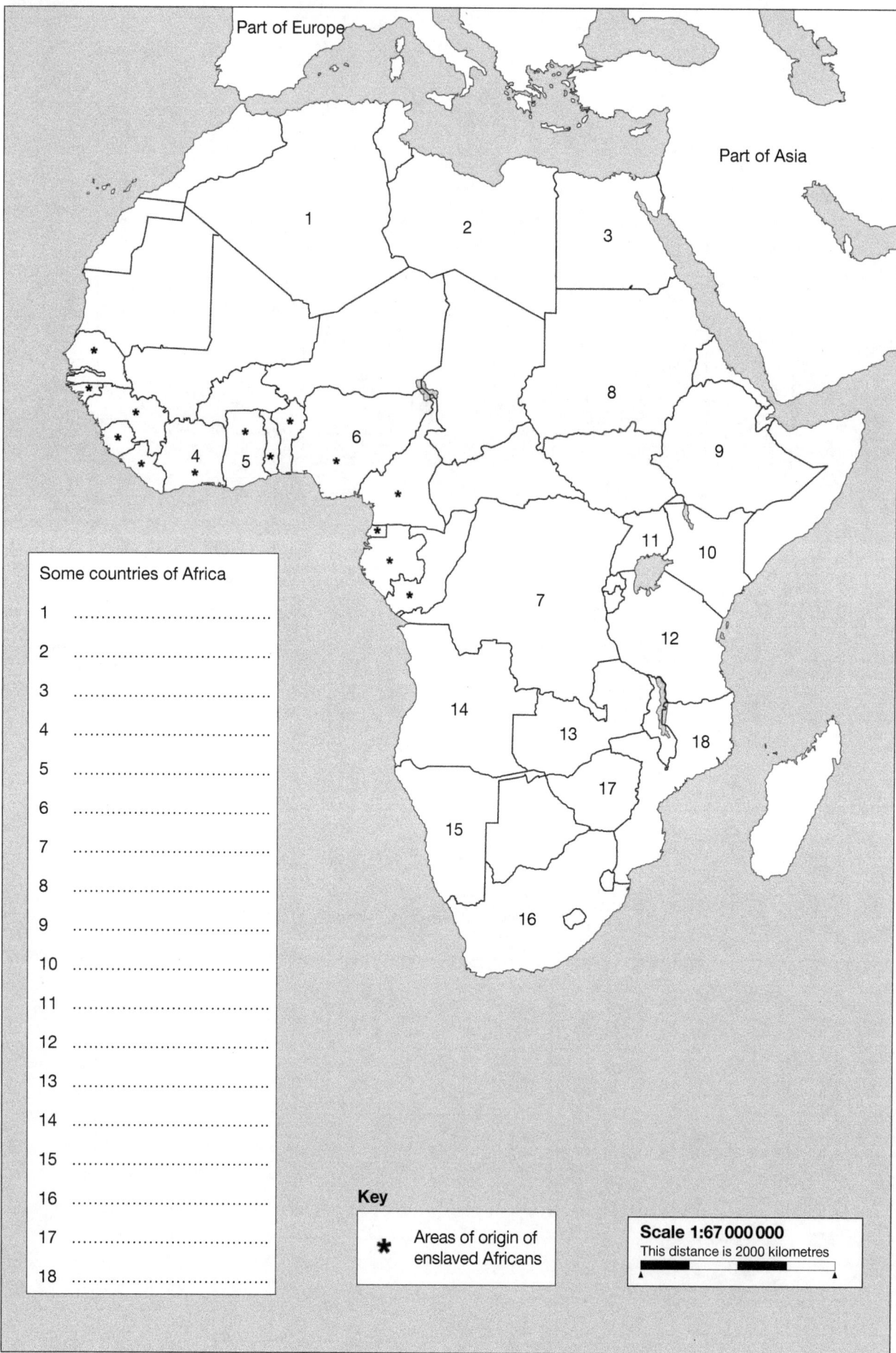

Present-day countries that were the origin of Africans transported to the Caribbean region